PALACES UNDER THE SEA

A GUIDE TO UNDERSTANDING THE CORAL REEF ENVIRONMENT

by

JOE STRYKOWSKI

and

RENA M. BONEM

photographs by Joe Strykowski

Library of Congress Cataloging-in-Publication Data

Strykowski, Joe.
    Palaces under the sea : a guide to understanding the coral reef environment / Joe Strykowski, Rena M. Bonem.
        p. cm.
    includes bibliographical references and index.
    Preassigned LCCN: 92-62290.
    ISBN 1-882533-00-3
    1. Coral reef ecology. 2. Coral reefs and islands.   I. Bonem, Rena Mae.   II. Title   III. Title: a guide to understanding the coral reef environment.

QH541.5.C7S87 1992   574.5'26367
                                        QBI92-20080

Printed in the USA

Published by
Star Thrower Foundation

cover art by Tom Lynch

"What fishes like flowers, what stones like trees. The coral reefs are a golden girdle of dead and living cities, which dwarf in their age and beauty all the cities of man."

— *Claire Booth Luce*

CONTENTS

LIST OF LINE DRAWINGS

LIST OF BLACK AND WHITE
PHOTOGRAPHS

LIST OF COLOR PLATES

Earth from space.

PREFACE

As astronauts soar along the great trackless boulevards of space, of all the spectacular vistas they are privileged to witness, none can evoke the heart tug of the sight of the mother planet, Earth. Anyone who has seen the unforgettable photographs of our great wandering planet has been struck by the undeniable fact that, at least from that magical perspective, Planet Earth might better have been named Planet Ocean. That extraordinary photograph, made from a point 10,000 miles out in space, confirms the vastness of our great oceans.

Any school child can tell you that 70.8 percent of Earth's surface is covered by oceans; yet sadly, few people have the vaguest idea of what percentage of the world's surface is covered by coral reefs. The answer is that coral reefs cover only about 1 percent of the ocean floor. One percent . . . and yet, these shimmering kingdoms created by tiny, flower-like marine animals are perhaps the most beautiful edifices on this planet.

In our short time on Earth, we have come to know intimately many natural features. Television, books, and magazines have brought the great mountain ranges, luxuriant forests, and the grandest of canyons to us. The beauty of these creations is enhanced in the knowledge that nature in its inexorable creeping of glaciers, cataclysmic upheavals, and endlessly running waters has sculpted from prehistoric magma a land mass of endless natural beauty.

The Grand Canyon, the Himalayas, the Sahara and all the world's natural and man-made structures cannot begin to match the coral reef in its beauty and wonderment - wrought not by the unseen, violent belching of the earth's molten core, but by the gentle growth of the most diminutive living creatures. The coral reef is a world formed by strange and prolific marine animals, more fascinating and potentially more important to man's continued survival than any other natural feature.

Coral reefs provide building materials and protection for coastal zones. They provide habitats for most of the diverse marine life abounding in tropic seas and provide limited food for many of the world's hungry. From coral reefs have come exciting new medicines to help in the fight against cancer, heart disease and many other illnesses, and let us not forget the incalculable benefits derived from the reefs as a source of tourist revenue around the world. In the Florida Keys alone the reef-related income is calculated as hundreds of millions of dollars annually.

The coral reef has been described as an underwater metropolis sheltering more kinds of life than any other oceanic community. Beneath the surface of the sea, all of the coral reefs of the world become as one, formed of a substance that we call "coral." Wrought by the combined efforts of underwater plant and animal life, coral is a substance composed of the skeletons of countless diminutive marine creatures. It is these primitive little reef builders that have erected for us a fantasy land of exquisite beauty. It is no more possible to describe a living coral reef than it is to describe a great work of art. To be fully appreciated, a coral reef must be experienced; not merely seen, but experienced.

It is necessary to understand the development and existence of the coral reef before its potential can be safely tapped, while at the same time insuring the preservation of the reef ecosystem. If we are to understand this most complex of marine ecosystems, if we are to understand the incredible longevity and stability of this fabulous world of glimmering gardens of living creatures, we have many questions to ask and many problems to solve. We have much to learn from the changing composition of the reef community, not the least of which is its extraordinary resilience in view of the drastically changing ocean environment.

For centuries adventurers have sailed tropic seas, returning home with tales of palm-fringed lagoons and coral grottoes glimmering beneath translucent turquoise waters. But not until the 1950s, with the development of recreational scuba diving, did serious first-hand scientific study of the coral reef begin.

Scuba, and more recently, the use of submersibles and ROVs, have provided this generation of scientists and others who have been fascinated and challenged by the mystery surrounding the world underwater, with tools so necessary for the study, so richly deserved, and so vital to the continued survival of the coral reef.

Reefs formed of coral are among the oldest communities on earth, having existed for over 200,000,000 years. A century ago, the nature of coral animals and the reefs they formed was a mystery to science. As little as 50 years ago, thousands of reefs flourished in warm tropical waters around the world. Today, the outlook is grim. The same coral reefs that have remained viable over enormous spans of geologic time and environmental change are now in great danger.

That coral reefs have survived and remained viable for so long is a tribute to the interdependence and symbiotic relationships within the reef ecosystem, yet their very survival belies the complexity and delicate nature of coral reefs. The world population has vastly overestimated the ocean's ability to withstand the abominable degradation of this sensitive environment. The last 10 years have seen a dramatic change in the world's coral reefs. Humans, in their short time on earth, have posed one of the greatest threats to the reef's continued existence in its long history. An insidious combination of lethal forces, including coastal development and dredging, dumping, pollution, collecting, fishing, boat groundings, anchorage, diving . . . and the growing threat of oil exploration and production . . . assaults coral reefs each day. As these planetary treasures, the world's coral reefs, die and are replaced by algal and sediment-covered rubble, we have only two choices.

We can, as we have done so often of late, turn our collective back on the problem . . . hoping futilely that the problem somehow has been overstated and ignoring the realities of hard facts. However, our legacy to yet unborn generations demands our best efforts. They deserve a planet with at least as much promise as the one we inherited. The future cries out to us. We must act now to limit our impact on the reef ecosystem immediately and to step up the fight to reverse the trend of decline. Our challenge with this book is to provide information and educational materials to heighten public awareness of the imminent dangers facing our reefs.

Shallow coral reef of the Red Sea.

CHAPTER 1

THE ORGANIC REEF

To the casual observer, a coral reef may be regarded as a stone structure rising from the sea floor. Those who have bothered to study reefs have learned that they are not, in fact, solid masses of conventional rocks. Rather, the reef is a unique biological community supporting many species in ecological balance. Today's once-living coral ramparts are sheathed in a living veneer of plants and animals.

Snorkelers and divers visiting coral islands marvel at the great coral battlements that have withstood centuries of storm violence coming from the vast blue tranquility of the sea. No less magnificent are the coral gardens that ring bright turquoise lagoons.

In tropic seas, the coral reef is an oasis in a blue marine desert. Within the shelter of its rigid framework of interlocking and encrusting skeletons of reef-building plants and animals there lives a diverse underwater community. The same warm waters that encourage coral growth attract a wealth of species. Colorful fishes, echinoderms, mollusks, crustaceans, and plankton all find refuge and sustenance within the reef. As we have so painfully learned, any interference with this balance can have a catastrophic impact on life in the sea.

What is a reef? The answer depends on whom you ask. To a lookout on an ancient Viking ship, a "rif" was a rib of rocks lying dangerously close to the surface. Since the "rif" posed a serious threat to the safe movement of his ship, the reef was a treacherous hazard to safe seafaring. Modern mariners have no less respect for the reef as a hazard to navigation. Any ridge of sand, coral rubble, or rock lying close enough to the surface that a vessel might ground upon or strike it is regarded as a reef.

Although we commonly ascribe the name "coral reef" to any reef built largely of stony coral, all reefs are not made of coral. In reality, reefs formed almost exclusively of coral are rare indeed. The calcareous algae and hydroids are equal in importance to corals in the growth and development of a reef. Still, the dominant and most spectacular feature of most tropical reefs are the stony (scleractinian) corals.

In warm tropical waters there are several types of living reefs that have no coral framework at all. These include the "worm reefs" composed of calcareous tube-building worms, vermetid reefs formed of worm-shaped snail shells, and mangrove reefs. The non-coral reefs are limited in distribution and their importance is relatively minor. Therefore, the focus of this book is on the coral reefs of the world, those that include the stony corals as a dominant element in reef-framework construction.

To the snorkeler and recreational sport diver, the coral reef is a magnificent underwater playground of iridescent living creatures amid grottoes and gardens of glimmering coral.

The businessman regards the economic potential of the reef. In the Florida Keys, for example, the revenue generated by reef-related tourism is estimated conservatively to be over $100 million a year. In 1986, 1.5 million visits were made to the reefs off Key Largo, Florida, by boat and airplane! The John Pennekamp Coral Reef State Park and Key Largo National Marine Sanctuary cover only 178 square nautical miles, including sea grass beds and mangrove swamps. Projecting such "reef economics" to the Great Barrier Reef complex of Australia, which stretches 1,300 miles along Australia's northeast coast and covers more than 79,000 square miles, boggles the mind.

To Charles Darwin and other early naturalists, the reef was a living organism formed through a complex association of plants and animals, and to reef scientists today, the reef stands as a dynamic ecosystem . . . a living structure whose rigid, wave-resistant ramparts modify and change the environment that surrounds it.

The reef's continued existence depends on suitable environmental conditions, including temperature, salinity, depth, water circulation, nutrients, and water quality. In this matter, the reef is not helpless; it is surprisingly capable of modifying its environment. Just as we modify our environment by adding central heating, air conditioning and shelter from severe weather, reef organisms modify their environment by uniting to construct dynamic, wave-resistant structures.

GEOLOGIC HISTORY OF CORAL REEFS

Throughout geologic history, reefs have come and gone in an endless cycle of life, death and renewal. Reefs have existed since life first began on Earth . . . more than 2 billion years ago. Corals appear to dominate modern living reefs, but that hasn't always been true. Reefs in the geologic past were formed by any living organism capable of producing a hard skeleton and anchoring to the sea floor. Ancient reef-builders included bacteria, algae, hard sponges, oysters, worms, and extinct hard corals. The evolution of early reefs into today's scleractinian coral reefs can be traced back more than 200 million years.

With enormous fluctuations in sea level during the past 2 million years came corresponding changes in the shapes of oceans and the paths of ocean currents. As the oceans receded, vast coral reefs were exposed to the atmosphere and died, leaving behind only limestone mounds, such as those that now form the upper and middle Florida Keys and other coral islands in the Caribbean, Atlantic, and Indo-Pacific. This occurred during the geologic epoch known as the Pleistocene or "Ice Age." At various times during this period, much of the Asian, European and North American continents were covered with immense glaciers. As the glaciers formed, enough of the ocean's water was trapped as ice to cause sea level to drop as much as 400 feet. Not until 18,000 years ago, when

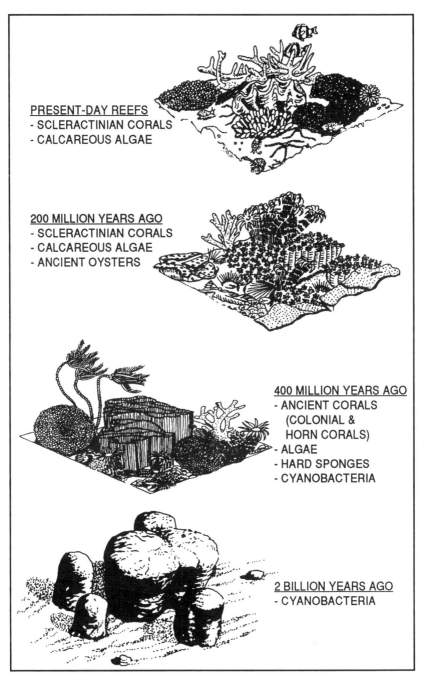

PRESENT-DAY REEFS
- SCLERACTINIAN CORALS
- CALCAREOUS ALGAE

200 MILLION YEARS AGO
- SCLERACTINIAN CORALS
- CALCAREOUS ALGAE
- ANCIENT OYSTERS

400 MILLION YEARS AGO
- ANCIENT CORALS
  (COLONIAL &
  HORN CORALS)
- ALGAE
- HARD SPONGES
- CYANOBACTERIA

2 BILLION YEARS AGO
- CYANOBACTERIA

Important tropical reef builders through time.

the glaciers began to melt, did the seas again begin to rise. About 9,000 years ago the sea had risen enough to cover the continental shelves, and the long-exposed ancient reefs became the bases on which today's living reefs developed. Only in the past 6,500 years has the rise in sea level slowed sufficiently to allow today's reefs to develop.

HOW REEFS ARE FORMED

In 1842 Charles Darwin described reefs as wave-breaking structures built by . . . "apparently insignificant creatures." He allowed, however, that these creatures were also responsible for the construction of a solid reef, "which day and night is lashed by breakers of an ocean never at rest." As recently as the late 1800s, it was commonly held that the "insignificant creatures" were *zoophytes*, invertebrate animals, which in appearance and growth patterns resemble plants.

Charles Darwin

Zoophytes were believed to construct reefs by stacking coral in mounds much the same as an ant colony builds an ant hill. Of course, Darwin and the other early naturalists learned quickly that the spectacular structures commonly called coral are, in fact, not formed by solitary individuals at all. Coral, the backbone of the reef community, is built primarily of calcium carbonate secreted by millions of tiny individual animals called polyps.

Thus, corals are far less like great boulders and much more like a microcosm of apartment complexes in which millions of coral polyps live together as a community. The diameter of a polyp can vary in size from the tip of a pin to more than 12 inches across. As a human needs a skeleton to protect internal organs and support soft tissues, coral polyps produce an external skeleton of limestone that becomes a protective shelter into which the polyps can retreat.

Polyps commonly feed at night by extending aggressive tentacles, which surround their mouths, into the water to catch plankton that the changing tides wash over the reef. The tentacles sting, trap, and force microscopic animals into the polyp's digestive system. Since corals have relatively few natural enemies under normal conditions, they are not heavily preyed upon by other animals.

The true reef-building corals are frequently called hard or stony scleractinian corals because of their ability to build hard skeletons of calcium carbonate. These corals are successful reef builders because they are remarkably adaptable. They can adjust to a wide range of conditions, and they can modify their size and shape to suit differing physical conditions, such as light and water energy.

The coral polyp is the sea's master mason. Depending on the coral species and sea conditions, the reef grows inexorably as the coral polyps deposit layer upon layer of limestone on the surface below their bodies. To the uninformed, the coral appears dead. To those who understand how the reef proliferates, the magic of living coral is in how the solid coral skeleton develops and becomes a reef, a haven for a kaleidoscope of life.

As each tiny coral polyp grows and multiplies, a transformation occurs. If you judge only by the bleached corals being sold in curio shops, you'd believe that corals are typically bone white. Although the limestone skeleton of coral is generally white, living corals come in a wide range of vivid colors. Small polyp-covered stones evolve into a multiplicity of convoluted forms, shapes, and colors.

Coral is the heart of the reef, the most vital component in the complex maze of living organisms and environmental conditions forming the reef ecosystem.

THE REEF ECOSYSTEM

Coral polyps and the biological community of which they are a part have unique biological significance. Perhaps the amazing proliferation of life forms supported by the reef has led to the extraordinary number of symbiotic associations that exist within the reef community.

The coral reef may support a greater diversity of plant and animal species than any other habitat on Earth. The reef is a complicated structure, physically and biologically. It has evolved after a long history of competition for limited resources of food and space. The health of the reef is delicately balanced. As the reef builds by the formation of limestone skeletons and the gathering of sediments, the destructive forces of nature are constantly at work. Hurricanes, boring worms, grazing animals and plants tear at the edifice.

Corals live in almost all of the world's oceans, but they can construct reefs only in tropical seas. Considering the vastness of the surface of Earth, reefs develop in a relatively narrow area of the oceans covering a mere 68,000,000 square miles. In this area, reef growth occurs only when conditions of suitable hard bottom at shallow depth, relatively constant water temperature (averaging above 70° F), and relatively clear, low-nutrient water of appropriate quality exist.

Consider carefully, the soft and gelatinous tissue of the coral polyp and the awesome power of the oceans. That the coral reef has withstood eons of such violent pounding and destruction tells us much about its tenacity, and yet, how much more is less widely understood.

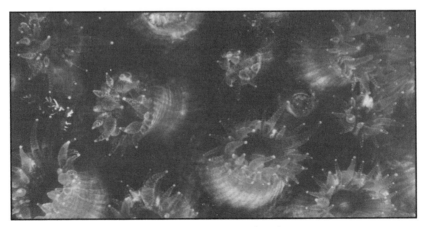

Cavernous star coral polyps.

Shallow coral reef of Andros, Bahamas.

CHAPTER 2

THE REEF COMMUNITY

The modern coral reef is built through "bio-construction," a euphemism for a process in which reef-building corals, along with algae, shells, and single-celled animals deposit the limestone that composes the reef. This limestone, the surrounding sediments, and the debris of other animals and plants are then cemented together by coralline

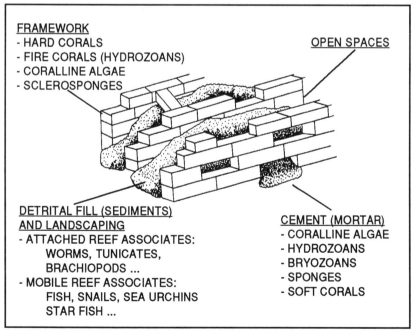

FRAMEWORK
- HARD CORALS
- FIRE CORALS (HYDROZOANS)
- CORALLINE ALGAE
- SCLEROSPONGES

OPEN SPACES

DETRITAL FILL (SEDIMENTS)
AND LANDSCAPING
- ATTACHED REEF ASSOCIATES:
    WORMS, TUNICATES,
    BRACHIOPODS ...
- MOBILE REEF ASSOCIATES:
    FISH, SNAILS, SEA URCHINS
    STAR FISH ...

CEMENT (MORTAR)
- CORALLINE ALGAE
- HYDROZOANS
- BRYOZOANS
- SPONGES
- SOFT CORALS

Reef components.

algae and encrusting animals. Irregular growth and bioerosion by marine organisms honeycomb the solid reef, creating space. The interaction of growth and erosion forms the coral reef by a process not unlike building a house.

ELEMENTS OF A REEF

Consider the house. Basic to its design are 1) bricks for the framework, 2) mortar to cement the bricks, 3) insulation and landscaping for the building, and 4) doors, windows, and rooms to provide living space. The reef components closely parallel those of the house. The reef has a framework, cementing organisms, sedimentary fill, and open spaces. Other plants and animals associated with the reef may be regarded as the landscaping and gardens cultivated once the house is in place.

THE FRAMEWORK

The master builders in the complex coral reef society can be counted on one hand. The reef framework must be strong enough to withstand destructive forces of hurricanes and heavy seas. Only a few organisms, reef-building scleractinian corals, coralline (limestone-secreting) algae, hydrozoans and, in deep water, sclerosponges, can be called primary frame builders.

Corals

Scleractinian corals (stony corals) form hard calcium carbonate skeletons, unlike the delicate, soft antipatharian and gorgonian corals, which leave no lasting structure when they die. Hermatypic corals, the reef-builders, differ from ahermatypic corals, the non-builders, in that hermatypic corals require tropical water and light for growth and formation of massive skeletons. Swarms of single-celled plants live within the tissues of hermatypic corals. These microscopic algae or zooxanthellae, are responsible for the ability of hermatypic corals to form reefs.

There are many symbiotic relationships on the reef, but the most important is the mutually beneficial association of hermatypic corals with the zooxanthellae living in their tissues. Symbiosis with zooxanthellae permits corals to thrive in the most nutrient-poor waters of the oceans. The zooxanthellae, too, would die without nutrients (nitrogen and phosphorous compounds) and carbon dioxide produced as waste products by the corals.

During the day, zooxanthellae harness the sun's energy through photosynthesis to convert waste products of the corals into oxygen and complex carbon-based molecules that can be used for food by the algae and the corals. Food produced by the algae during the day supplements plankton captured by coral polyps at night. The corals utilize this food for respiration and produce more wastes, which are used by the algae to produce more food.

Cavernous star coral of Jamaica.

Large numbers of zooxanthellae are embedded in the tissues of each coral polyp. If severely stressed, the corals can expel the zooxanthellae . . . or even feed on their algal guests.

At the genesis of its life, each coral polyp begins to secrete lime, usually on top of old limestone skeletons. The zooxanthellae assist the coral polyp in building its skeleton by removing ammonia and carbon dioxide from the water. If not removed, these chemicals would interfere with skeleton formation. In this way, large apartment complexes of living corals develop as the animals divide and grow.

Coralline Algae

Coralline algae are as important as corals in the construction of the reef framework. In deep water, cold water, or areas of heavy wave action, the limestone skeletons secreted by coralline red algae may be the only reef framework capable of growing.

Hydrozoans

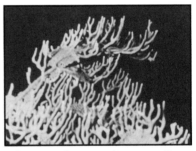

In shallow water, the reef may be constructed almost entirely of *Millepora*. *Millepora*, commonly known as fire coral, is not a scleractinian coral. It is a hydrozoan, which is a close relative of the true corals (anthozoans). (Both the anthozoans and hydrozoans belong to the large group of animals called cnidarians.) *Millepora*-built frameworks can be quite impressive, particularly in shallow waters, where conditions do not favor scleractinian corals. If a reef is destroyed through extreme turbidity, excessive sedimentation, or the grounding of a vessel, *Millepora* is commonly the first framework element to colonize the old-reef surface.

Fire coral encrusting sea fan.

Sclerosponges

In deeper water (below 200 feet) or in dark tunnels and caves, the reef framework may be comprised primarily of sponges with a hard, coral-like internal skeleton. Because sclerosponges grow slowly, they cannot compete with the faster growing corals, hydrozoans, and calcareous algae of the shallow reef, where sunlight promotes photosynthesis by zooxanthellae.

MORTAR

In order to create a wave-resistant structure, the reef framework must be bound together physically by cementing organisms. The role of these binding organisms, including the red coralline algae and the encrusting fire coral *Millepora*, is at least as important to the construction of the reef as mortar is to the building of a house. As the bricks of a house are cemented together with mortar, so too are the dying framework elements of the reef bound together by coralline algae and *Millepora*. In this way, as polyps die, their skeletons are joined together to form thick crusts that unite the isolated framework elements.

Reefs commonly grow fastest in shallow water, where heavy algal crusts are directed toward the sun and the highest wave action occurs. Although they also can act as primary-framework elements, coralline algae and *Millepora* primarily function as binders of the reef's external surfaces. To a lesser degree the reef is further strengthened and protected from erosion by the direct chemical precipitation of calcium carbonate.

Other animals may play a role in the cementation of the reef. Encrusting colonies of single-celled animals (foraminifera) often are found under coral heads and ledges. Irregular aggregates of coiling calcareous-tube worms and a host of lesser creatures are also cementers. Encrusting snails, ahermatypic corals, soft corals, other hydrozoans, oysters, bryozoans (moss animals), and brachiopods (lamp shells) all help to build an enormous variety of reef structures.

SEDIMENT

Although the main reef-framework components are the scleractinian corals and coralline algae, surprisingly over 70 percent of the calcium carbonate in the reef is composed of sand particles and debris of even finer grain sizes. The sediments, which support and provide a foundation for the reef, are classified as skeletal (derived from reef organisms) or non-skeletal (derived from other sources).

Skeletal Infrastructure

Most of the reef sediment comes from the reef organisms. When the plants and animals associated with the reef die and their tissues decay, their skeletons may break apart and accumulate on the bottom as skeletal sediment. This sediment is typically the size of a grain of sand and may include fragments of foraminifera, clams, snails, sea urchins, brittle stars, star fish, sea lilies, fish, crabs, and sponges.

Certain algae (red, green, and brown) have calcium carbonate skeletons and resemble higher plants, but lack true roots, stems, and leaves. Such calcareous algae produce vast amounts of sand and mud-size sediment when they die. In addition to the mud produced by fine, calcareous algae, spicules of sponges, soft corals, and sea cucumbers may be ground into tiny crystalline sediments. How far and wide these sediments are spread depends on the energy of the waves, currents, or organisms doing the transporting, and to a lesser degree . . . the size, shape, and composition of the sediment itself. Additional skeletal sediment may accumulate by physical or biological erosion of the reef structure.

Physical erosion of the reef occurs when fragments of the cemented reef framework are broken from the reef by heavy seas. The broken material produced in this way is known as "reef rock." It includes the rubble of scleractinian corals, algae, hydrozoans and other skeletal sediments that have been cemented together. Over the course of time, this rubble may be fused together with the nucleus of other reef builders to form a massive framework.

The solid infrastructure of the reef is constantly being eroded by reef organisms, a process that is vital to the health of the reef. This bioerosion creates living space in the heart of the reef and forms skeletal sediment that, when cemented, forms reef rock.

Non-Skeletal Material

Although most of the sediment associated with reefs is skeletal, non-skeletal sediments can be significant along coastal areas where the shoreline or river outflow may contribute vast amounts of terrigenous (land-derived) materials. In addition, in lagoonal or shallow areas, ooids, pellets, and clasts eroded from older limestones and salt or other chemical deposits may be important.

Sediment Zonation

Reef scientists describe sediments by size and composition, which is determined by the environment's physical and biological properties. The plant and animal life as well as the sediment deposited on or near the reef are controlled

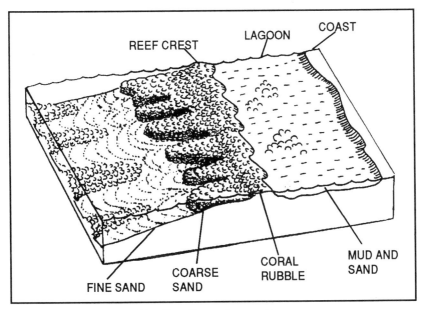

Reef sediment zonation.

by nutrient supply, topography and geography of adjacent land, relief of the sea floor, oxygen supply, mean temperature and salinity, water depth and light intensity, circulation patterns, water energy, and sedimentation rates.

Sediments may be distributed into distinct zones created by variable water energy, location of the sediment source, and original sediment composition and durability.

The location of the sediment source determines what materials are available. The nature of the original material determines the final sediment size and composition. Consider the skeletal fragments of corals, clams, snails, coralline algae, larger foraminifera, sea urchins, and calcareous worms. They are typically the size of a grain of sand or larger because their skeletal structure does not break down easily into finer sediment. This sediment is generally found on the shallow forereef, on the seaward side of the reef crest, where wave energy is moderate.

As might be expected, the coarsest sediments are deposited in areas of maximum wave energy, at the reef crest or along the shoreline. Finer sediments (spicules of sponges, soft corals, and sea cucumbers, fragmented skeletons of green algae, smaller foraminifera, and bioeroded mud) are found in either calm lagoonal water or on the deep forereef.

OPEN AREAS

A multitude of boring organisms, from simple bacteria, fungi, algae, and sponges to complex marine worms, sea urchins and clams, is constantly at work honeycombing the stony heart of the reef. An estimated 40 to 70 percent of the reef consists of tunnels, grottoes, and caves. Within these spaces lives an extraordinary variety of plants, corals, and other animals. The nooks and crannies provide a unique habitat, offering protection from predators and environmental extremes of light, temperature, water energy, salinity, and desiccation. The dark recesses within the reef also may provide a safe, shallow-water habitat for deep-water, light-sensitive organisms. In this way, it is possible for light-dependent, shallow-water scleractinian corals and algae to live side by side with deeper water organisms in spite of different requirements.

Reef scientists classify reef cavities by shape, size, origin, and illumination. Some of the largest spaces are open vaults formed between massive coral heads or submerged caverns shaped on land during an ancient period of lower sea levels. Many of the smallest cavities include skeletal voids or vacated borings within coral skeletons. Because light intensities vary from well-lighted to very dark areas, the plants and animals found in these spaces differ from one cavity to the next. The reef is filled to capacity!

Perhaps it is this richness of diverse biologic species, all overcrowded into a relatively small reef, that has created the pressure among reef dwellers to formulate the intimate relationships we witness on today's reefs. Even as worms, clams and sponges bore their hideaways into the coral, they weaken it. This porous limestone is rendered more susceptible to destruction by violent wave action and eventually crumbles. New colonies spring from the ruins of their ancestors and other great coral cities grow upward and outward. The open areas of the reef are as important to the reef community as the windows, rooms, and doors of a house to its human inhabitants.

Moray eel, a typical cavity dweller.

Larger reef spaces produced by irregular growth (Red Sea).

CHAPTER 3

REEF CLASSIFICATION

The traditional axiom of geology, "the present is the key to the past," is the basis for today's knowledge of past reefs. Because coral reefs grow slowly, many scientific theories regarding the formation of reef complexes are the result of deduction and inference. Encircling the tropics of both hemispheres are coral reefs, magnificent monuments to the continuity of life. No matter where on Earth they may be, all coral reefs develop certain common forms.

HISTORY OF REEF CLASSIFICATION

Nearly 150 years ago, Charles Darwin proposed that three kinds of coral reefs exist: fringing reefs, barrier reefs, and atolls, all related in their geologic history. Darwin had traveled extensively in South America and his observations of the geology of the Andes had led him to the belief that upheavals of the Earth's crust created mountains in one area, and its subsidence caused valleys and basins in others. His travels across the Pacific reinforced his belief that the formation of coral reefs was attributable to the same geologic phenomena. Darwin observed that the outside walls of coral reefs fell away to great depths, but living corals existed only where sunlight penetrated the water. The critical question became, "from what deep foundation do the reef-building corals grow?" He concluded that the three reef types were merely different stages of reef development around a gradually sinking volcanic island.

Darwin's Conclusions

Darwin believed coral reef formations were caused by three processes: 1) submarine volcanos formed islands rising from the sea floor; 2) after these islands rose above sea level, they gradually began to sink back into the sea; and 3) as the islands subsided, their coasts were colonized by coral polyps, which thrived in the sunlit, shallow waters.

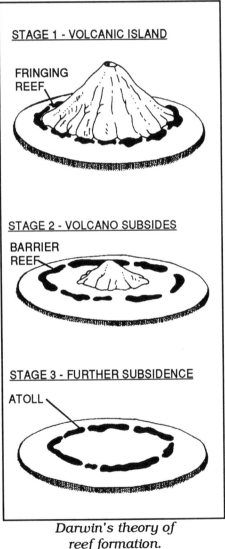

According to Darwin, the fringing reef was the first to form. It developed around the shallow coast of a newly emerged volcanic island. As the island subsided, perhaps because of volcanic eruption and subsequent loss of lava, the reef directed its growth upward toward the sun to maintain its position with respect to sea level. As new polyps grew on top of the skeletons of their predecessors, the distance between the reef and shore increased, forming a lagoon and associated barrier reef. Darwin felt that the lagoon formed because nearshore growth was inhibited by large amounts of sediment being eroded

Darwin's theory of reef formation.

from the subsiding island, or by the presence of less oxygen and food than available on the seaward side of the reef. Eventually, the entire island submerged and only a circular atoll with a central lagoon remained.

Darwin's Submergence Theory has been supported by substantial evidence of subsidence from published reports of the DEEP SEA DRILLING PROJECT and other investigations. For example, in the 1952, drilling on Eniwetok Atoll in the Marshall Islands found volcanic rock under more than 4,000 feet of coral-rock layers. Similar drilling on Midway Atoll in 1960, discovered a volcanic core nearly 1,300 feet below sea level. These examples provided clear and undeniable evidence of ancient volcanic islands, upon which untold generations of coral reefs had grown.

Although Darwin's theory remains essentially valid today, Darwin himself would be the first to remind us that it is oversimplified and incomplete. The reality of submergence is beyond question, but submergence may result from processes other than those suggested by Darwin. Only a few Caribbean reefs are related to volcanic islands. Many of the Pacific's fringing reefs, barrier reefs, and atolls appear to have no basis in volcanism, nor do most of the Atlantic reefs.

Modern Refinements

Darwin's theory is even more impressive considering that he proposed the theory long before he had ever seen a true coral reef. Amazingly, the sum of his first-hand experience examining living reefs was only 12 days. Darwin lacked knowledge of the sea-level changes of the Pleistocene Epoch and plate tectonics, both of which have added measurably to our understanding of coral reef formation and distribution.

Glacial Activity

Other scientists relate the formation of barrier reefs and atolls to sea-level changes resulting from the glacial activity of the Pleistocene Epoch. This differs considerably from Darwin's submergence theory. Its proponents believe the foundations of modern reefs were formed during the last Ice Age. Because a large amount of sea water was trapped in glaciers on land, sea level was significantly lower. This resulted in the formation of erosional terraces upon which modern reefs developed.

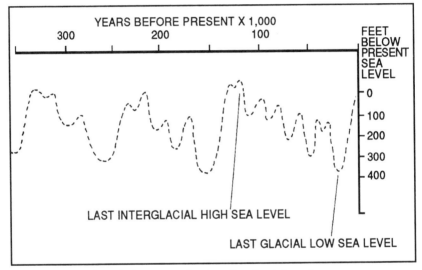

Sea level changes during the last two ice ages.

The evidence supporting the Glacial Activity Theory was based on the discovery that the flat floors of lagoons appeared at the relatively uniform depth range of 150 to 270 feet throughout the Pacific. The theory was further reinforced by the discovery of cliffs and terraces underwater similar to those formed by waves along rocky shores. The flat terraces indicated three distinct drops in sea level: 400 feet, 110 feet, and 55 feet. Each of these drops represented one of the last three phases of glacial activity during the Pleistocene Epoch. It is noteworthy that these depth ranges are consistent with glaciologists' estimates of sea-level changes during the Pleistocene. The eroded terraces were submerged as the glaciers melted and sea level rose. These hard surfaces formed an ideal substrate for new reef growth.

Like Darwin before them, the proponents of the Glacial- Activity Theory lacked knowledge of plate tectonics. They failed to recognize that in recent history, reefs have gradually submerged and re-emerged throughout the Caribbean and the Indo-Pacific through a process that had little to do with volcanic subsidence or glacial activity. It was, instead, a result of the tilting, uplifting, and sinking along the margins of tectonic plates.

Plate Tectonics Theory

As recently as the 1960s, the scientific community was generally comfortable with the belief that the continents and great-ocean basins of Earth were permanently fixed in position relative to one another. Then, because of new data about the sea floor, some natural scientists began to pose highly controversial questions. Was it possible, for example, that the continents of Africa and South America had been one land mass at some earlier geologic time? Could

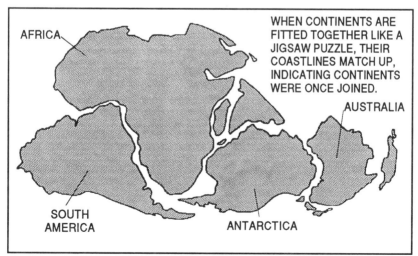

Former position of southern continents.

some enormous force have divided the continents and set them drifting apart?

Tectonics, geologically speaking, is the study of the deformation of the Earth's surface. The term, plate tectonics, relates seafloor spreading to the movement of major plates that make up the Earth's crust. According to the plate tectonics theory, these crustal plates are moved by sub-crustal-convection currents in the Earth's upper mantle. Molten lava rises at oceanic ridges as underwater volcanos producing new oceanic crust. This crust spreads outward from the ridge and down into the

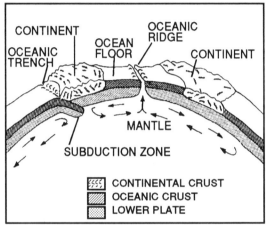

Cross section through earth showing plate tectonic movement.

mantle at oceanic trenches. The plates may converge, diverge, or slide past one another.

The Caribbean and the Indo-Pacific are complex regions of significant tectonic movement. Some areas rise in response to lateral seafloor spreading, while other areas fall. The resultant tilting causes an emergence of ancient reefs from the sea where the Earth's crust is rising and conversely, submergence of ancient reefs where the crust is sinking.

In addition to tectonic history, Caribbean reefs differ from Indo-Pacific reefs in another way. Caribbean reefs have experienced retarded growth patterns since the last Ice Age. It has been proposed that the rapid rise in sea level, proximity to nutrient sources, and cooler temperatures in the smaller ocean basin have combined to produce less well-developed reefs in the Caribbean, a theory not uniformly accepted by all reef scientists.

Currently, reef formation is best explained through a combination of theories: Darwin's subsidence of volcanic islands, glacial activity, and plate tectonics. But how about coral reefs that form with no apparent subsidence or sea-level change?

Antecedent-Platform Theory

Given the proper water depth and the appropriate water conditions, almost any terrace or bank can form a foundation for reef growth, without subsidence or sea-level variation. Reefs, given favorable conditions, will grow regardless of the geologic history of their substrate. The ultimate morphology of the reef, however, is inextricably linked to growth relative to sea level.

MORPHOLOGIC CLASSIFICATION OF REEFS

If reefs seem to have been difficult to define, they appear to have been equally difficult to classify and subdivide judging by the many different criteria used. The heart of Darwin's theory still provides the most satisfactory classification. Reefs are classified by their shape (morphology) and relation to land, a system that is simple to understand and easy to apply to reefs anywhere. The size of a reef, the water depth, and other criteria are appropriate standards for the subdivision of basic reef classifications.

Reefs occasionally have been classified by their geologic history (evolution), but this is a complex process. The accurate interpretation of reef evolution is difficult, making a classification system very complicated. Such a classification needs a high degree of specificity and as a result can rarely be applied beyond the area of its development. Using Darwin's basic classification by reef morphology and relationship to land, reefs are described as: fringing reefs, barrier reefs, atolls, and patch reefs. To Darwin's original classification is added the bank (platform) reef, which forms on top of shallow rises or platforms on the continental shelf.

Fringing Reefs (Shore Reefs)

Coral reefs vary greatly in size and shape, but the most accessible, and consequently the easiest to study are those lying close to shore. Fringing reefs grow parallel to shorelines where suitable hard bottom can be found. Equally necessary are favorable conditions including abundant sunlight and warm, shallow waters. Any excessive runoff of fresh water, nutrients, and sediments onto the reef will interfere with healthy development of the corals. Where sediments are abundant (river outflows and construction or dredging sites, for example), reef development is patchy.

The upward growth of corals and associated reef life is controlled by sea level, but lateral reef growth is determined by the topography of the sea floor. Sheer walls and steep dropoffs will support only a narrow band of corals, whereas broad horizontal growth can occur on a wide platform.

Fringing reefs typically support only a veneer of boulder corals, star corals, or brain corals. Finger corals and fire corals grow on the rocky rubble near shore. Frequently, branching corals may form in a narrow zone seaward of the reef crest.

Reef areas that are being gradually submerged over a period of several thousand years develop thick layers of reef deposits. As the sea floor gradually subsides, the coral organisms continue their upward growth, depositing increasingly thicker layers on the reef base. In the waters of the Red Sea, Hawaii, and south Florida, where reef history is long, the thickness of the reef deposits is likely to be significant.

Environmental conditions permitting, fringing reefs develop around most continents and islands of the Indo-Pacific and the Caribbean. That is not to suggest, however, that corals can grow anywhere in these regions. On some shores, excessive wave action, freshwater runoff, nutrients, and shore-generated sediments preclude the development of healthy coral reefs. On Australia's Great Barrier Reef complex, fringing reefs grow around many of the high islands, such as Magnetic Island or Lizard Island, where the continental margin is a broad, shallow shelf. Australia, traditionally however, is best known for its barrier-reef development.

Barrier Reefs

A barrier reef is a linear structure separated from the shore it parallels by a lagoon. It typically develops along the seaward edge of a platform or shelf extending from shore. Although the top of the reef or reef crest is quite irregular, the area between the reef and land, the back reef, slopes gently into the lagoon. The lagoon floor is typically covered with land- or reef-derived sediment and is spotted with irregular patch reefs. Surge channels, formed by wave erosion and irregular coral growth, sculpt breaks in the barrier reef, resulting in spur-and-groove systems on the seaward side of the reef or forereef. Channels are also formed as extensions of submerged river valleys on land.

Off Australia's northeastern continental shelf lies the Great Barrier Reef complex, including the world's most spectacular group of barrier reefs. Although the reef is regarded as the largest barrier reef in the world and appears to be a continuous wall extending nearly 1,300 miles from north to south, it is in fact a complex of more than 2,900 coral reefs formed along the shelf margin.

The northern Great Barrier Reef is dominated by "ribbon reefs." These are narrow, elongated barrier reefs which can be as wide as 1,500 feet and as much as 15 miles long. Living corals edge the outer ramparts of the barrier reef, while sediments settle on the gentle slope of the lagoonal margin.

No other reef in the world can compare with the Great Barrier Reef complex in its enormity, and yet, there are barrier reefs in the Caribbean that are equally magnificent. The Belize Barrier Reef is more than 124 miles long, the longest in the Atlantic and the second longest barrier reef in the world; and adjacent to the Tongue of the Ocean on the Atlantic side of the Bahamas Archipelago lies the barrier reef off Andros Island. There are other barrier reefs in the Caribbean, smaller still, that are slowly evolving from fringing reefs as sea level rises.

Bank Reefs

When sea level rises so rapidly that barrier reefs are unable to maintain their position relative to sea level, bank reefs develop. In contrast to barrier reefs that form on the shelf margin, bank reefs rise from the continental shelf and lie on submerged hills or platforms (which are themselves limestone remains of more ancient reefs). These reefs can grow large enough (with areas as great as 260 square miles) to support coral islands (cays). Examples of bank reefs that form a barrier-like complex are the outer reefs of the Florida Keys. Lagoons formed behind bank reefs tend to be shallower than those behind barrier reefs. Similarly, the forereef profile of the bank reef lacks the steepness of the barrier reef.

Atolls

Darwin noted that atolls were rings of coral reef forming on the tops of subsiding ancient volcanic islands or sea-mounts rising from the sea floor. Not all atolls have the nearly perfect oval shape seen in classic aerial pho-tographs. More

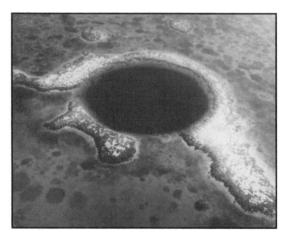

Caribbean atoll, Lighthouse Reef, Belize.

commonly, the atoll's shape reflects the seafloor topog-raphy. When an atoll forms around a submerged volcano, it is likely to be circular.

Atolls also vary substantially in dimension. Some atolls are less than 1 mile across; others are more than 20 miles in diameter. The outer ramparts of the atoll are formed of calcareous algae and slope steeply to the deep-ocean floor. Coral spurs and sediment-filled canyons project over the seaward margin and drop onto gently sloping, sediment-covered terraces. This form indicates significant vertical growth. Behind the algal ridge lies the reef flat and the lagoon. Lagoonal patch reefs are common in the quiet water and depths may range to 200 feet.

Since Darwin's time, it has been generally held that atolls formed around submerged volcanos, a belief supported by the distribution of atolls. Atolls are uncommon in most of the world oceans, but they are found in large numbers in the Indo-Pacific because of the greater number of submarine volcanos than elsewhere. Other atolls appear to form when ribbon reefs are exposed to a dominant wave direction. Still others, like those of the Maldives in the Indian Ocean, demonstrate sea-level changes on a low carbonate platform. The central lagoon fills with sediment as the sea-level falls, causing the emergence of low, circular, coral islands. The outer rampart of the atoll is encrusted with a purplish algal ridge that grows rapidly to sea level, forming a circular rim.

Not nearly so well known nor as numerous as those of the Indo-Pacific, but quite beautiful in their own right, are the coral atolls of the Caribbean. As well developed as those in the Indo-Pacific, Caribbean atolls are protected by ridges of fire coral in the same manner as the algal ridges protect the atolls of the Indo-Pacific. Probably the two best known Caribbean atolls are Glover's Reef and Lighthouse Reef off Belize. Numerous atolls lie along the Mexican coast including Alacran Reef. The Bahamas Archipelago also has a number of atolls (Hogsty Reef is one of the most famous). In addition, Albuquerque Cays, Courtown Cays, Roncador Bank, and Serrana Bank lie off Nicaragua.

Reef scientists, geologists and biologists alike, have named and defined several smaller reef types. The names of these reefs are usually linked to the shape or origin of the reef.

Patch Reefs

Small reef formations growing on shallow shelves or on lagoonal floors are called patch reefs. These reefs commonly grow inside the outer reefs and are commonly surrounded by sea grasses. Coral knolls are small, isolated lagoonal mounds of coral that rarely grow high enough to be exposed by low tide. Coral knolls may have diameters greater than 1 mile.

A pinnacle reef is another form of lagoonal reef that takes its name from its shape. It is a spire-shaped coral reef that features an abrupt, vertical rise from the lagoon floor. Still other patch reefs are named for their physical features: hill, bowl, and wreath reefs being only a few.

Lesser Reefs

Table reefs are small reefs that rise from the deep-ocean floor, but have no relation to any larger structure and no lagoon. Faros or atollon are small, ring-shaped, coral reefs that have a shallow central lagoon. They are commonly associated with the rims of larger atolls or barrier reefs and are found in the Bahamas Archipelago and the Maldives.

Micro-atolls are enormous single coral heads or groups of coral heads, growing in shallow water and having a diameter that ranges from 3 to 25 feet. Micro-atolls typically consist of an outer edge of living coral surrounding a dead center. They are created when the surface of the coral is destroyed by rain water at times when the top is exposed during exceptionally low tides. The sides of the coral, which are submerged, are protected and continue to grow upward. This results in a rim of live coral surrounding a low, dead center.

CHAPTER 4

CONTROLS ON REEF GROWTH

Reef-building corals thrive in shallow tropical seas where sunlight is abundant. The distribution of living coral reefs is limited by the availability of the specific environmental conditions required by the diminutive coral animals. For example, reef-building corals rarely live deeper than 200 feet and then only if the water is clear and the temperature remains above 68° F.

DISTRIBUTION OF CORAL REEFS

The warm water band in which coral reefs can develop girdles the Earth, wandering only about 30° north or south of the equator. Although some corals are tenacious enough to grow in surprisingly turbid water, most corals will suffocate under heavy sedimentation. Consequently, clean water is vital to healthy coral development. Moving water is another requirement; through tidal shifts and wave action, life-sustaining oxygen and nutrients are carried to coral polyps.

Sunlight is one of the most important requirements of growing corals, for the algae, living within the tissues of the coral polyp, demand sunlight for photosynthesis. These algae help provide oxygen for the coral and assist in eliminating the coral's wastes. Prolific coral growth occurs only within a very narrow range of environmental conditions.

ENVIRONMENTAL REQUIREMENTS

Early studies described coral reefs by their shapes or morphologies and their relationship to fluctuations in sea level. Only recently have coral reefs been related to the physical and biological aspects of the environment. To understand the distribution of reefs one must first understand the environmental conditions required for reef growth. Because reefs are so widely distributed throughout tropical and subtropical environments, reef builders (and their associates) are considered to be resilient creatures. In reality, they exist only in a delicate balance. Survival depends on all vital environmental factors being in absolute harmony.

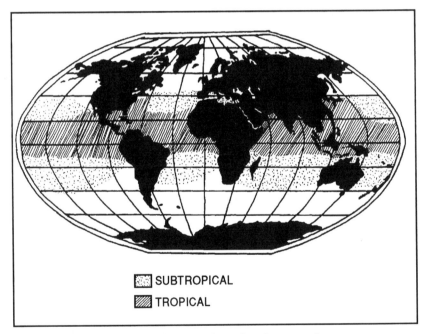

SUBTROPICAL
TROPICAL

Distribution of tropical and subtropical zones in the world oceans. These zones correspond to areas of potential coral reef development.

Temperature

Of the parameters governing the building of coral reefs, none is more critical than temperature. Coral animals cannot thrive and develop reefs in waters colder than 68° F. Although coral reefs cover more than 1,560,874 square miles throughout the world's tropical and subtropical seas, the most spectacular reef development occurs where the mean annual water temperature is 74 to 78° F. Only a few corals can survive temperatures as low as 57° F or as high as 86° F. Most healthy corals can manage temperatures as low as 65° F for brief periods. On the other end of the spectrum, temperatures ranging from 90 to 100° F have been recorded in shallow pools with little apparent impact on corals, but these are the exceptional corals and certainly not representative of the average. It is important to note that no significant coral reefs develop where temperatures are consistently outside 68° to 83° F.

Although a few species of coral survive at temperatures considerably above or below the optimum, such reefs grow slowly. Lower temperatures interfere with coral reproduction and growth, and higher temperatures hamper the feeding process and may be related to oxygen toxicity.

In the Atlantic Ocean, reefs develop best on the east coasts of continents. Prevailing cold currents on the west coasts preclude coral growth, with the exception of a few African reefs. The northernmost limit of healthy reef development is south of Miami, Florida. Again, it is noteworthy that exceptions do exist. Where the Gulf Stream Current passes the island of Bermuda, its warm waters encourage some limited reef development; and a few reef-building corals survive as far north as Cape Hatteras.

In the Florida Keys, reefs develop best where protected from the cold, turbid waters flowing out of Florida Bay. During the winter months, the bay's cold waters kill important reef-building elkhorn and staghorn corals. Cold temperatures are fatal to the larvae of most reef-building corals.

Additionally, recent evidence links high temperatures to the coral "bleaching" phenomena of 1983, 1986,

1987, and 1990 throughout the Pacific and Atlantic Oceans. Precipitated by an extended period of calm, hot weather, the symbiotic algae were expelled from the coral polyps. The result was the color fading (bleaching) of the polyps, reduced food supply, and diminished ability to deposit skeletal material. Although much of the stressed coral survived, there was a high rate of mortality.

Light

The reef's biological productivity is, to a large extent, tied to sunlight. The symbiotic photosynthetic zooxanthellae, living within reef-building corals use sunlight to produce food that is shared with the corals. This food supplements zooplankton captured by the corals, and in fact, some coral polyps can live for years without feeding because most of their energy requirements are satisfied by food provided by these tiny single-celled algae. If abundant light is a fundamental building block of healthy reef development, the absence of light is a limiting factor.

Although water turbidity decreases available light, one significant factor limiting light is water depth. As depth increases, the amount of sunlight absorbed by the water increases. Thus, the depth to which sunlight can penetrate is one factor determining coral zonation on the reef. For example, mounding or boulder-shaped coral heads grow in shallow waters where sunlight is abundant. Conversely, flattened plate corals develop at greater depths.

Since an estimated 60 percent of sunlight's energy is absorbed beyond 30 feet, it is not surprising that the greatest diversity of species and their maximum growth rate occur in depths less than 30 feet. Reef corals grow at greater depths, but

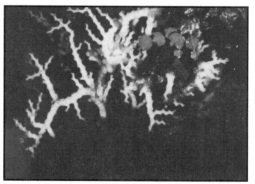

Ivory bush coral lacks zooxanthellae.

they grow best in shallow water. In fact, hermatypic corals can be found in water depths as great as 120 to 150 feet, and a few corals have been discovered by research submarines as deep as 510 feet, where the amount of sunlight is much less than 3 percent of the surface illumination. At these depths, however, the corals are not significant reef builders. Corals without zooxanthellae can be found in any sea and at depths as great as 17,500 feet!

Turbidity results from suspended particulates diffusing, reflecting, and absorbing sunlight and converting it to heat energy. Because turbidity severely restricts sunlight penetration, it is a major control of coral growth. The vertical water transparency is determined by using a Secchi disk, a large, circular plate painted in alternating quadrants of black and white. When the disk is lowered into the water to the limit of visibility, readings of 13 to 105 feet are common in the Florida Keys. However, following storms and heavy rains, turbid runoff from Florida Bay can produce readings of 0 feet! Therefore, reefs of the Florida Keys are best developed where protected from this turbidity.

Emersion

Although it is undeniably true that most corals cannot live out of water, a few Caribbean corals do survive briefly above water during low tide. Such corals as starlet coral (*Siderastrea radians*), rose coral (*Manicina areolata*), mustard hill coral (*Porites astreoides*), brain coral (*Diploria clivosa*), and golfball coral (*Favia fragum*) are examples that can survive a few hours above water. Low tides severely restrict growth of other Caribbean corals.

Indo-Pacific corals, by comparison, seem to tolerate exposure better, and in places like Heron Island on the Great Barrier Reef, the entire reef crest may be exposed at low tide for several hours. Tolerance to exposure may have developed because of the great differences between high and low tides on the Great Barrier Reef, where spring tides are often as great as 33 feet.

Salinity

Coral reefs develop best in waters where the salinity or salt content of the water ranges from 35.0 to 38.0 parts per thousand (ppt). This is not to suggest that corals won't grow outside that range. Some of the world's most beautiful corals live in the Red Sea, where salinity averages 40 ppt. However, most corals show a decided preference for salinities at or near that of average sea water (34 to 36 ppt).

There are many corals, however, that can survive salinity extremes (from lows of 17.5 to highs of 52.5 ppt). It is not surprising that those corals hardy enough to survive brief periods of emersion are also able to tolerate the extremes of salinity attendant to heavy rain storms (low salinity) and lagoonal or tidal pool evaporation (high salinity). The keys to survival for these species seem to be 1) length of emersion, 2) temperature, and 3) inadequate rainfall to substantially decrease tidal-pool salinity.

Corals that can tolerate brief emersion are protected from the sun's desiccation by a mucus secreted by the polyp. This slippery secretion, along with water retained on the coral's irregular surfaces, moistens and protects the delicate coral animal from drying and from extremes of salinity.

Oxygen

Reef waters are commonly saturated with dissolved oxygen (90 to 125 percent) during the day. Maximum levels of dissolved oxygen may reach 250 percent (or more) of saturation during mid-afternoon, when photosynthesis of plants is at its peak in shallow, brightly lighted waters. In restricted pools this level can fall to less than 18 percent of saturation at night. These levels of oxygenation are well within the tolerance range of reef organisms.

The pH (acidity) of sea water is closely related to coral metabolism and the amount of dissolved oxygen. As a rule, it does not limit reef growth. Seawater values range from slightly alkaline (8.9 pH) to slightly acidic in areas of high evaporation or poor circulation. Average seawater in reef areas has an acidity of 8.2 - 8.4 pH.

Nutrients

Understanding nutrients in general, and specifically the significance of low-nutrient levels in sustaining coral growth are the two most important advances in coral studies in the last decade. For nearly 100 years, reef biologists have known that coral reefs are well developed where nutrients (phosphorous, ammonia, and dissolved nitrates) are not abundant. The reasons for this appear to be arguable.

Some scientists compare the low-nutrient content of reef waters to nutrient levels in a desert, and others feel that the variety of life on the reef results from intense competition for food. As we have grown more environmentally aware, we have recognized that the coral framework of the reef can be destroyed when nutrient levels are elevated unnaturally. The destruction is directly related to increases in the growth of algae, fungi, and bacteria.

When the reef ecosystem is overloaded with nutrients, the result is eutrophication. Nutrient overloading may occur through an upwelling of nutrient-rich bottom waters or shifting water currents sweeping more nutrients over the reef. Gradually rising sea level, sewage outfalls, groundwater seepage, land run-off of fertilizer (or other nutrients) are all culprits. Perhaps the first sign of trouble may be the development of band

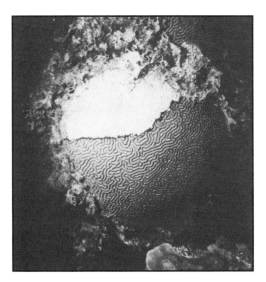

Band disease, Andros, Bahamas.

disease on some branching corals or head corals. In the worst case, the surface of an entire reef may be covered by algae, bacteria, and fungi. As nutrient levels increase, coral reefs may well become dominated by algae and bacteria.

The success of reef-building corals in shallow water with low-nutrient levels has been related to the zooxanthellae, the microscopic dinoflagellate algae living in the tissue of hermatypic corals. It was formerly believed that the primary function of zooxanthellae was to add oxygen to the reef waters, and that they provided little food for the host coral. A secondary function - it was held - was to remove waste products of coral metabolism and stimulate coral calcification (deposition of coral skeletons) by modifying water chemistry.

It is now recognized that zooxanthellae transfer 95 to 98 percent of the photosynthetically-produced carbon to the host coral! As long as there is sufficient sunlight to enable the zooxanthellae to produce food by photosynthesis, few corals need to feed actively by day. Even so, most corals are active night feeders and are very effective in trapping and retaining prey. Using tentacles, cilia, and mucus nets they trap zooplankton (copepods, amphipods, foraminifera, and larval snails, clams, hydroids, and polychaete worms), juvenile fish, and suspended organic matter.

The reef can consume nearly all the organic material it can produce. The coral framework offers not only shelter, but even food for other reef organisms from bacteria to sponges.

Water Circulation

Reefs thrive on moving water. Circulation must be adequate to bring in limited nutrients and oxygen and take away waste products. The impact of circulation on reef growth is an observable phenomenon. Note, for example, that the maximum reef development typically occurs on the windward side of the reef. Occasionally, wave energy is so violent (during a tropical storm, for example) that the reef and its inhabitants may be physically damaged.

The zonation of reef corals is determined by water energy as much as by sunlight. Caribbean elkhorn coral (*Acropora palmata*) has a stout branching shape and is ideally suited to growth in the breaker zone. Elkhorn coral directs the growth of its sturdy branches into the waves to disperse the wave energy. Other branches are broken off, resulting in the colony becoming "wave oriented." Staghorn coral (*Acropora cervicornis*) conversely is far more delicate and thrives best where sheltered, in deeper or quieter waters. This beautiful and prolific coral takes its name from the antler-like shape of its branches. Because it is as fragile as glass, it is often decimated by tropical storms. It is not uncommon, after a particularly violent hurricane, to find a great rubble pile of dead staghorn on the windward side of the reef. Periods of abnormally high- or low-wave energy also can impact the reef organisms by altering water transparency and sedimentation patterns.

Sediment

Sediment refers to the particles of rock or skeletal debris that accumulate on the bottom and may be suspended in the clearest looking water. It can impact the development of a coral reef in several ways. Any sediment, depending on its concentration and the size of the particles, will reflect and scatter sunlight as it travels through the water. Where sedimentation is heavy, turbidity is increased and sunlight is reduced drastically. Photosynthetic activity of zooxanthellae and other reef plants is severely restricted. As a consequence, the coral is weakened and the deposition of reef-building calcium carbonate is limited. An interesting result of decreased light penetration is that deeper water organisms are able to move into waters much shallower than they could normally tolerate.

Heavy sedimentation also can suffocate reef organisms. When reef areas are covered by sediment, the organisms that survive are those able to throw off the sediment. Those that cannot remove the sediment are quickly smothered under it and die. Some corals are tenacious and remove the sediment as quickly as it accumulates. Still other corals have adapted to the removal of a particular size of sediment and successfully throw off the sediment using tentacles, cilia, or mucus nets, but the energy required to remove the sediment weakens the coral. If corals are already stressed or weakened by nutrient excess, they may be readily smothered by sediments.

Some corals have developed unusual ways to eliminate sediments. Pillar corals, branching corals, and domed corals shed sediments by virtue of their shapes. Pacific mushroom corals are solitary, unattached corals that remove sediments by inflating their carpet-like surface with water. If that fails, these acrobatic corals have been witnessed executing somersaults, a highly effective method. Large polyps of star coral can pump water to eject sediment from their surfaces, and some corals have cilia or sweeping tentacles, which are extended day and night to remove sediment. Some star corals and brain corals use mucus nets to eliminate sediment.

Reef development often occurs in response to protection from sedimentation. In the Florida Keys, for example, reef growth occurs primarily where the reef tract is protected by islands or keys. Only a few major reefs have developed where directly exposed to the heavily sedimented waters of Florida Bay, and today these reefs are near death. As a practical matter, the stability of the substrate in areas of rapid sedimentation may be more important than the reef organisms' ability to remove sediments.

Substrate

For a coral polyp to grow, it must first be firmly anchored to a suitable substrate. The substrate must be hard and stable, and free of shifting sediments. To survive, the free-living coral larvae must settle in protected cracks and crevices. When the sea floor is covered by mud or other bottom sediments, potential settlement zones for the larvae are limited. Before it can be a strong base for coral development, a sandy or muddy bottom must be stabilized.

Filamentous blue-green bacteria can bind sediment particles together to form a tough, leathery mat or stromatolite that will support the growth of reef organisms.

The bottom topography itself influences coral growth. It has been suggested that flat substrates are typically colonized by mounding corals or massive head corals; bottoms with slight relief or slope will be settled by branching corals; and plate corals and encrusting corals will inhabit the steep slopes.

Sea-Level Changes

Sea level profoundly affects the shape and distribution of coral reefs. Massive reef development occurs when the rise in sea level is sufficiently slow that upward growth of the reef is able to maintain the same relative depth. When sea level rises too rapidly, however, the reef may not be able to hold its relative position. As a result, the reef organisms unable to survive in the greater depths are destroyed.

Conversely, as sea level drops, the reef organisms must move into deeper water. If they cannot, they must either adapt to shallower water or be destroyed by emergence and slowly deteriorating water quality.

Rising sea level also can affect the reef indirectly by increasing nutrients due to nutrient release from newly flooded lands. It is believed that this may be happening in the Florida Keys, where rising sea level could be contributing to the destruction of reefs.

Clownfish living in anemone seems unaware of sea level rise in the Maldives.

Red Sea lionfish.

CHAPTER 5

LIFE AND DEATH OF THE REEF

Every natural community progresses through a series of developmental stages before reaching maximum potential. When all environmental elements for coral reef growth are in place, how does reef genesis occur?

REEF BEGINNINGS

Coral reefs, like most other marine communities, develop through a series of predictable stages. As might be expected, they are dominated at any particular time by the organic group favored by the environmental conditions of the moment. Typically the stages include periods of surface preparation, colonization, competitive diversification, and maturity.

Colonization

Before a coral reef can take root and grow, the sea floor must be prepared. When covered with loose, muddy or sandy sediment, the substrate must be stabilized and made "erosion-proof." Cyanobacteria (blue-green algae) and other algae bind the sediment into a tough, leathery mat in the same way that grass binds soil. In a different way, hard substrates are also prepared for colonization. Boring organisms (bacteria, fungi, and algae) can drill holes into hard limestone surfaces to accommodate colonization.

After the surface has been prepared, pioneer organisms (plants and animals) are attracted to the substrate and begin to colonize the sea floor. Pioneer colonizers frequently include hydrozoans (like *Millepora*, the fire coral), encrusting coralline algae, sponges, soft corals, and sea anemones. Less frequently, the colonizers may include finger corals, small solitary corals, and "golf ball" corals. These diminutive corals do not add significantly to the building of a wave-resistant framework.

Patch reefs form as new substrate becomes available for colonization. Given the right environmental conditions, and sufficient time, patch reefs develop into transitional reef communities, and eventually into major bank reef communities.

Diversification

As a diverse group of plants and animals begins to colonize every available space and exploit every food source, a true wave-resistant framework develops. The structure is then regarded as a coral reef, providing habitat and food for a wide variety of highly adapted organisms.

Depth, bottom conditions, and wave energy determine which major, framework corals will be present. Plate corals, pillar corals, brain corals, star corals, and the branching corals are typical framework builders. Even as the framework and cementing organisms are building the reef, boring and grazing organisms are eroding its foundations.

Maturity

As the coral reef matures, specialization of the community increases until the number and variety of organisms living on the reef reach their theoretical ultimate potential, the "climax community." Since environmental conditions are seldom stable long enough to allow potential diversity, a true climax community rarely exists in the marine world. Instead, cycles of high and low diversity occur, corresponding to periods of environmental change and stability.

When the environment is undergoing constant change, the community is likely to be dominated by a few opportunistic organisms. Such opportunists thrive and reproduce during ideal conditions and survive less favorable conditions (increased turbidity, high nutrients, significant temperature shifts, salinity change). Unfavorable conditions typically result in a shift toward an algae-cyanobacteria-dominated community.

CORAL REEF GROWTH

The development of a coral reef is most easily described by examining the growth of the primary framework builder, the hermatypic scleractinian coral. The coral larva (planula) is a tiny, free-swimming animal that may search for days for an unoccupied protected crack or crevice in which to settle and grow. The planula selects the location carefully based on physical conditions and placement offering competitive advantage over other organisms.

After it has selected and settled upon a suitable substrate, coral growth begins. Even after settling, however, the planula is at high risk because of its size and may be overgrown or attacked and eaten by fish, sea urchins, or other predators. The coral colony started by the planula is subject to changes in the physical and biological environment (such as sea level and temperature variations). Certain corals adapt to particular environments and are greatly stressed by any environmental change. For example, free-standing, fragile branching corals are commonly found in sheltered lagoons or quiet tidal pools. They typically form thickets in shallow water, where sunlight is the most abundant. However, they cannot survive the breaking waves or storm energy at the reef crest because intense wave energy will destroy their fragile skeletons. At the reef crest, only the massive boulder corals weighing as much as several tons, or the stout palmate corals, can thrive and dominate the fauna.

In deep water, where sunlight penetration is minimal, corals are dominated by flat, platy corals with characteristic thin skeletons. Deep-water corals frequently have large polyps, although this may be a shallow-water coral's adaptation to heavy sedimentation.

The ability to tolerate changing environments is a trait of some corals. Species of *Porites*, for example, can appear as delicate finger coral on one part of a reef and as a thick, encrusting coral on a shallow part of the same reef. Most coral species, however, have narrow environmental restrictions. Altering the environment at the very least slows the development of these corals, and in the worst case, destroys them.

Growth Rates

Current studies indicate that the branching corals are the fastest growing corals. Of the Caribbean's major reef-framework builders, it is staghorn coral, *Acropora cervicornis*, that grows most rapidly. Growth rates of up to 10 inches per year have been recorded for this coral in Jamaica. In the Florida Keys, where water temperatures are near the lower limits for its growth, *Acropora cervicornis* grows only 4 inches per year and the stout elkhorn coral, *Acropora palmata*, about 2 inches per year. However, in spite of slower growth, elkhorn coral forms a major part of the shallow-reef framework in the Florida Keys because it is less vulnerable to storm damage than the more fragile staghorn coral. Like all other organisms, corals do best under optimum conditions.

The star coral, *Montastrea annularis*, is the most common coral in the Caribbean. It forms

Slow-growing cavernous star coral.

boulders with diameters of 5 feet or more. Because of its massive shape, skeletal material must be added on all sides as it grows. As a result, boulder corals grow much more slowly with an estimated annual growth rate of 0.2 to 0.4 inch per year. Fortunately for the reef, this common boulder coral withstands all but the most severe storm activity.

At these growth rates, a reef 150 feet thick could, theoretically, be formed by staghorn coral in only 1,800 years. Conversely, star coral would need more than 7,200 years to achieve the same growth. Such estimates assume the absence of any destructive forces, a highly unrealistic assumption. All corals, especially staghorn corals, are susceptible to physical and biological destruction. Any meaningful growth-rate measurement must balance growth against destruction.

Growth vs. Destruction

A growing body of evidence suggests that coral reefs may grow faster after periods of unfavorable conditions. A reef with a history of sustained healthy growth has achieved biological stability, a favorable balance with its physical environment. It is inhabited by diverse corals well adapted to their respective positions within the reef. To maintain this harmony and balance, coral growth may be exceptionally slow. If the substrate slowly sinks, or sea level slowly rises (as it has since the last Ice Age), the reef will grow upward rapidly or slowly enough to maintain a position constant with sea level.

Following reef destruction by hurricanes in the Florida Keys and the Persian Gulf, researchers have documented rapid regrowth of staghorn corals, star corals, and brain corals. Swift development of filamentous cyanobacteria, hydrozoans, and alcyonarian (soft) corals has been observed where an entire reef has undergone catastrophic destruction, even requiring the substrate to be re-prepared and re-stabilized. Following stabilization, the substrate was quickly recolonized.

However, if the reef community is to survive, reef growth must exceed reef destruction. On many of the world's reefs today, the living coral appears to be only a thin veneer growing a mere few inches each year, barely keeping the reef from being destroyed by physical and biological forces.

NATURAL DESTRUCTION OF THE REEF

The natural processes that destroy the reef are physical, biological and chemical. Although any of these processes may occur independently, reef destruction results most often when one or more of the processes are combined. At the site of destruction, it is becoming increasingly rare not to see evidence of human influence.

Mechanical Breakdown

Although biological activity may undermine an entire reef and make it vulnerable to physical destruction, the external surface of the reef is the primary target of mechanical breakdown. Storm activity, heavy wave action, pounding surf, and strong currents break, tumble, and grind down vulnerable parts of the reef framework. The fast-growing branching corals are easily broken by violent wave action. Some researchers suggest that staghorn coral breakage may be, in fact, a major form of asexual reproduction. Yet massive breakage, as occurred in Jamaica in 1980, when Hurricane Allen roared across the island, can cause breakdown and death of the reef framework.

The ability of broken coral fragments to survive is variable. Large chunks of framework may be formed from coral, coralline algae, or hydrozoans that cannot survive further division. However, given a chance, they demonstrate surprising resilience and the ability to grow again. Whole shells of foraminifera, tiny snails, clams, and oysters are often found and can survive quite well.

Biological Destruction

Organisms can strengthen the reef framework by cementing and encrusting, or they can aid in destroying the reef by rasping, boring, or spreading bacterial decay. Many organisms bore into the reef in search of food and protection. Borers prefer substrates of dead coral and commonly invade the underside of head corals. Undermining the structure of the reef are boring algae, fungi, sponges, clams, oysters, sea urchins, barnacles, and polychaete and serpulid worms. Boring may be mechanical or chemical, or a combination of chemical secretion and mechanical rasping. As the framework becomes riddled by borers, the weakened substrate crumbles easily.

Many sea creatures take sustenance from the external surface of the reef. Snails, fire worms, starfish, sea urchins, sea cucumbers, crabs, and turtles join a myriad of fish in causing the external destruction of the reef by rasping away at the living coral tissue. Some of the finest sediment in the lagoon results from the endless rasping by parrotfish, which ingest astounding quantities of living coral polyps and their surrounding skeletal carbonate daily. Once the living tissues have been digested, the finely ground carbonates are expelled in a string of loosely packed fecal pellets. When nutrient supplies increase and coral health and

Parrotfish with beak-like mouth.

growth decrease, it is possible for "bioeroders" to destroy a reef faster than a healthy reef can grow. In some cases, bioerosion is accelerated by other destructive processes.

Chemical Solution

Although chemical destruction traditionally has not been high on the reef protectionist's list of imminent concerns, studies of Jamaican lagoonal reefs and Kaneohe Bay in Hawaii, demonstrate the importance of chemical solution in controlling reef shape and biota. Conditions of low pH, low carbon dioxide or carbonate-ion concentrations, low water temperature, and depth facilitate the removal of bottom materials. The impact of chemical dissolution may be significant particularly in areas where freshwater springs flow from a collapsing reef substrate.

CATASTROPHIC MORTALITY

The potential for the catastrophic death of coral reefs is well documented. Foremost among the reef destroyers are the recurring hurricanes and typhoons, which tear relentlessly at the seaward ramparts of the reef, smashing the reef crest's branching corals into fields of rubble. Enormous boulders of coral are physically displaced and tumbled across the sea floor. Torrential rain storms can flood rivers, pouring fresh water onto the reef, diluting the sea water until the coral organisms and other reef dwellers die.

Human-induced sedimentation from mining, dredging, or coastal development can precipitate an extraordinarily swift decline in water quality and the consequent mortality of the coral polyps. Abrupt changes in tides or sea level result in the death of reef inhabitants by the emersion or the drowning of the reef. It is clear that the mass mortality of reef animals and plants is caused by abrupt changes in the physical or biological environment, whether induced by nature or by humans.

Rain Storms

During heavy tropical rains, the salinity of shallow-ocean waters can be abruptly and substantially altered. "Rainy season" storms commonly damage coral reefs through decreased salinity and increased nutrients and sedimentation. The extent of damage ranges from the relatively minor (mortality of only the uppermost coral surfaces) to the catastrophic (death of the entire coral reef community). Serious damage also can result from abnormally low tides as coral organisms are unprotected from extremes of rainfall and temperature.

Hurricanes

The never-ending battle between the forces of creation and destruction is intensified in tropical and subtropical zones. It is ironic that these areas not only foster the growth of coral reefs, but also the development of hurricanes and cyclones. The impact of such storm activity on coral reefs has been well documented during the past 20 years.

Unquestionably, hurricanes and cyclones have produced the most severe reef damage caused by natural elements. In addition to the heavy rain, which dilutes seawater salinity and facilitates the movement of sediment, these storms commonly bring high-velocity winds that cause abnormal surge, flooding, heavy wave activity, and freak tides. Branching corals are smashed and bulldozed leeward, while the massive head corals - though more resistant to damage - may be ripped from the sea floor and rolled in the surge, crushing everything in their paths.

Predation on injured corals is heavy and widespread. The ocean water surrounding the reef is often fouled with excess nutrients and dead and dying organisms. This fouled water itself can destroy what plant and animal life may have survived the mechanical destruction and turbidity. Corals that are not killed outright may be so severely stressed that they become "bleached" because of the loss of their zooxanthellae.

The good news is that no matter how much damage has been done to reefs by hurricanes, reefs have rarely been destroyed completely by them. These storms may actually clean over-growing algae and sediment from the reef, allowing rapid regrowth of corals. Considering the severity

Storm damage, Great Barrier Reef.

of damage, and the proximity to other reefs, recovery times of 2 to 25 years are not unusual.

Earthquakes

It is clear that changes in salinity or sedimentation can have a destructive impact on life on the coral reef. Earthquakes also have the potential to cause catastrophic mortality of reef organisms. In addition to direct breakage of coral colonies, earthquake-generated movement can raise or lower reefs beyond their survival ranges. Seismic activity also can trigger catastrophic sea waves and submarine mud slides, resulting in coral breakage and sudden deposition of sediment. Besides the obvious smothering of the reef by sediments loosened by seismic activity, dams holding back reservoirs of fresh water on land may be ruptured with the predictable impact of millions of gallons of fresh water flooding the reef.

Thermal Stress

The records are filled with numerous reports detailing winter coral kills, especially in the Florida Keys reef tract. Corals are sensitive to temperature shifts and can easily be weakened or killed by extremes at either end of the scale. It is not surprising that the cold waters flowing from Florida Bay during the winter can injure or destroy the corals of the Florida Keys, inasmuch as these corals already live at the limits of their cold temperature tolerance. However, in most areas, reef organisms are living closer to their upper thermal limits, and small increases in temperature may be more lethal than temperature decreases. High temperatures may provide the key to understanding coral "bleaching" events.

Bleaching

The 1980s appear to have been the decade heralding yet another threat to the health and welfare of coral reefs, the phenomenon of "bleaching." Records demonstrate that coral bleaching events have been observed and recorded at least since 1977, and probably earlier. Corals are bleached because individual coral polyps expel their zooxanthellae, resulting in white or pale patching over the surfaces of the affected corals. When zooxanthellae are expelled, the coral is weakened and may die within weeks.

During the late summer of 1987, there occurred what has become known as the "Caribbean mass bleaching event." The phenomenon was unusually widespread, and included areas of the Florida Keys and much of the Caribbean. It has been suggested that a correlation exists between this and a similar bleaching event that had occurred earlier in the year (January through May) on Pacific Ocean reefs.

Although definitive explanations are still forthcoming, it appears bleaching events have some common elements. High water temperatures seem to be one associated factor. Still another factor is that all bleaching events have been preceded by periods of exceptionally stable weather, specifically periods of calm winds and calm seas.

Exposure to unusually high levels of light may stimulate overproduction of oxygen and cause the expulsion of zooxanthellae from colonial carpet anemones (zoanthids), brain corals, star corals, and shallow plate corals. Corals in deeper water or areas protected from high ultraviolet radiation were also affected. Certain sponges even lost their pigmentation.

Plausible explanations are numerous, but there is considerable difference of opinion. The Caribbean mass bleaching event at various times has been correlated to abnormal currents related to an "El Nino" - Southern Oscillation event in the Pacific and to warming due to the Greenhouse effect. There remains much work to be done.

Infestations

To study any coral reef is to gain an appreciation for the relation between the reef community and the physical and biological environment. It is a relation of extreme complexity and delicate balance, a critical balance that must be maintained in the never-ending struggle between the forces of growth and destruction.

When all parts of the reef ecosystem are in balance, coral growth exceeds destruction due to predation. However, the potential for coral destruction by infestation is very real. Any human interference, no matter how apparently insignificant, can cause a shift in balance between the constructive and the destructive processes on the reef. As in every realm of nature, with life and death always in conflict, when destruction outweighs construction, the result is disaster.

Crown-of-Thorns Starfish

The best documented infestation of coral reefs centers on a prickly, multi-armed starfish known as the crown of thorns, scientifically named *Acanthaster planci*. As recently as the 1960s, this spiny "multipede" was considered a shy, nocturnal reef grazer by the few reef scientists who knew it at all. However, this enigmatic starfish suddenly underwent a phenomenal population explosion, filling coral reefs throughout the Pacific with coral-killing marauders.

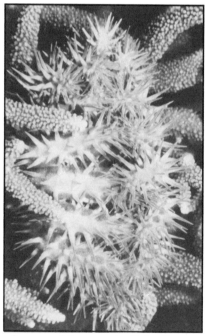

Crown-of-thorns starfish, Guam.

On Guam alone, in 2 1/2 years the crown of thorns ate its way through 24 miles of the island's reef, destroying more than 90 percent of the corals. On the Australian Great Barrier Reef, large-scale destruction caused by millions of these predators left behind only whitened coral skeletons stripped of all life. Nearly 25 percent of the 1,300-mile

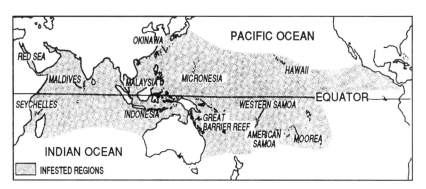

Distribution of crown-of-thorns starfish.

length of the Great Barrier Reef was infested and ravaged by the voracious predator.

Although a juvenile crown of thorns eats only algae, an adult, which commonly measures 10 inches across, can graze an area of coral twice its own diameter in a single day. Because of their incredibly high reproductive rate, populations can multiply by 100,000 to 1,000,000 times annually. The outbreak of crown-of-thorns infestations has been likened to forest fires. Within 2 or 3 days of the destruction of the corals, algae and bacteria begin to cover the surface, effectively preventing the growth of new corals. Later, as soft corals and sponges overgrow the hard surface, a new substrate forms on which a new generation of coral reef may grow.

At first, it was feared that humans collecting the spiraled Pacific triton shell had precipitated a decline in the crown of thorns' natural predators. However, recent findings of *Acanthaster* spines in ancient reef sediments indicate that population explosions occurred in the geologic past, before humans had a chance to alter the nature of their world. Nevertheless, the Pacific triton is one of the few natural predators of this formidable starfish and its numbers are steadily declining because of overcollecting.

In the early 1970s, bounties were offered in Australia to encourage the harvesting of the crown of thorns. Divers learned quickly that *Acanthaster* could be destroyed either by spearing or by injecting the starfish with formaldehyde. By 1977, the Great Barrier Reef exhibited no signs of starfish infestation, but, in less than 10 years, it - along with coral reefs in Japan and Micronesia - would undergo a new outbreak of *Acanthaster planci* infestation.

A growing body of evidence supports the theory that the increasing frequency of outbreaks is related to high levels of nutrient-enriched waters created by coastal runoff during heavy rains. These vastly enriched nutrient levels are thought to foster increased phytoplankton concentrations, which are, in turn, fed upon by the crown-of-thorns larvae. The additional food results in greater survival rates, as the juvenile grows rapidly to maturity and can produce 65 million eggs each year. Considering the appetite of the adult crown of thorns, the prognosis is not good.

Human efforts to contain the spread of the crown of thorns to date have met with little success. The massive agricultural use of fertilizers and widespread land clearing and deforestation projects underway around the coastal areas of the tropics and subtropics are clearly related to the increase in coastal sedimentation and nutrient enrichment. We must learn to curb our greed if we are to limit the flow of nutrients into coastal waters.

Nature, without human interference, probably controlled the crown of thorns very well in low nutrient waters in the past. In spite of its enormous appetite, the starfish is surprisingly fragile and can be easily broken and destroyed in heavy surge and wave activity. It will die if caught exposed during unusually low tides.

A concern has surfaced among Caribbean researchers. If the Panama Canal is ever expanded and enlarged to sea level, it is feared that it is only a matter of time before *Acanthaster planci* crosses into the increasingly nutrient-rich waters of the Caribbean.

Spiny Sea Urchin

Diadema antillarum, the long-spined, black sea urchin, had as long as anyone could remember, multiplied and thrived throughout the Caribbean and the Florida Keys. In February of 1983, without warning, a mysterious blight swept through this part of the world, destroying all but 1 percent of the *Diadema* population.

Though far less understood than the crown-of-thorns infestation, the extraordinary die off of the black spiny urchin had a dramatic effect on the coral reef community. The disease spread so quickly that reef scientists were caught unprepared to attempt to control or limit its consequences.

The removal of this benthic marine herbivore has had a major impact on Caribbean reefs. The loss of *Diadema* has caused an increase in abundance and productivity of reef algae. Algal cover has inundated large areas of reef, killing the coral framework by overgrowth and shading. In addition, loss of *Diadema* with the corresponding increase in algal cover has resulted in increased grazing and bioerosion of the reef by fish.

The crown-of-thorns infestation and the algal growth following loss of *Diadema* are but two examples of the tipping of the fragile balance that exists in the reef ecosystem. To preserve the reef ecosystem, we must keep all the elements in balance. If we are to maintain that balance, we must first understand the interrelationship of reef organisms.

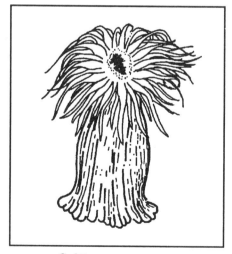

Solitary anemone.

CHAPTER 6

REEF DWELLERS, THE FRAMEWORK BUILDERS

Tide-washed coral reefs defend the inner lagoon from the fury of ocean waves. Seaward of the reef, snow-white breakers beat against submerged coral ramparts, while leeward, in emerald-green waters, a barely known world of living creatures propagates and thrives.

Before we can pretend to understand how to protect the coral reef, it is vital that we have some knowledge of the plants and animals that construct the primary-reef structure, the framework. A coral reef, it has been said, is like a catacomb of countless, long-dead creatures. Their limestone skeletons form the main building blocks of the reef.

Although we have discussed the endless work of countless generations of coral sculptors, each fashioning its own delicate legacy of lime, we know the reef is not a result of the polyp's labor alone. Many others have helped to create the coral reef, and the reef community is a natural habitat for millions of creatures that find within it safe refuge from a hostile sea. They are the stony corals, the fire corals, and the coral-like algae and sponges.

CORALS

Looking very much like a flower, with its branching fronds and multi-colored tentacles, it is no wonder that the

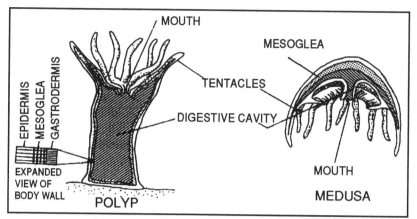

Two body forms of the Cnidaria.

individual coral polyp was long mistaken for a plant. Not until 1723 was it first suggested that coral might, in fact, be an animal rather than a plant. Coral is the common name given to some members of the Phylum Cnidaria. Cnidarians include hard corals, soft corals, fire corals, black corals, pipe-organ corals, feather corals, sea fans, wire corals, and sea whips, as well as sea anemones and jellyfish.

"*Cnid*" is a Greek word meaning stinging nettle and, since these animals all contain stinging cells or cnidoblasts (which contain nematocysts), they are called cnidarians. Phylum members may be colonial or solitary and may take one of two body forms, the polyp or medusa. Polyps are bottom dwellers and typically resemble the sea anemone with its sack-like body and mouth surrounded by a circlet of tentacles. The medusa, conversely, floats like a jellyfish, with mouth and tentacles extended downward. In both, the mouth opens into a "blind" digestive cavity.

Before the phylum was renamed Cnidaria, it was called Coelenterata. Referring to the animal's large digestive cavity, "coel" means hollow and "enteron" means gut.

Anatomy

The animal is composed of two distinct cell layers. The outer protective skin is the epidermis, which forms a funnel into the gastrovascular cavity. The gastro-dermis (the inner digestive tissue layer) lines the stomach. The meso-glea, a jelly-like mass of cells, lies between the epidermis and the gastrodermis. The me-dusa has much more of this jelly-like sub-stance, hence it is com-monly called a jellyfish.

*Cross section through
scleractinian coral polyp.*

Fleshy folds of gastrodermal tissue that divide the inside of the polyp into pie-shaped segments are called the mesenteries. They extend from the mouth to the base of the gastrovascular cavity. Between the mesenteries in stony corals are the septa, thin calcium carbonate partitions that strengthen the coral skeleton. Thread-like mesenterial filaments extend from the free edges of the mesenteries. These filaments are composed of digestive cells and are important for feeding and protection.

Classification

The Phylum Cnidaria is divided into four classes: the Class Scyphozoa, the Class Hydrozoa, the Class Cubozoa, and the Class Anthozoa. These divisions are based on the forms that the animal takes during its lifetime, and whether it lives most of its life as a polyp or medusa.

The term "alternation of generations" describes the cnidarian's extraordinary reproductive process with sexu-ally-reproducing generations alternating with asexually-reproducing generations. Alternation of generations as-sures wide dispersal and survival of offspring, while main-taining the continuity of the species.

A member of the Class Scyphozoa (the jellyfish), for example, lives most of its life as a medusa. The male and female medusae reproduce in traditional sexual union of

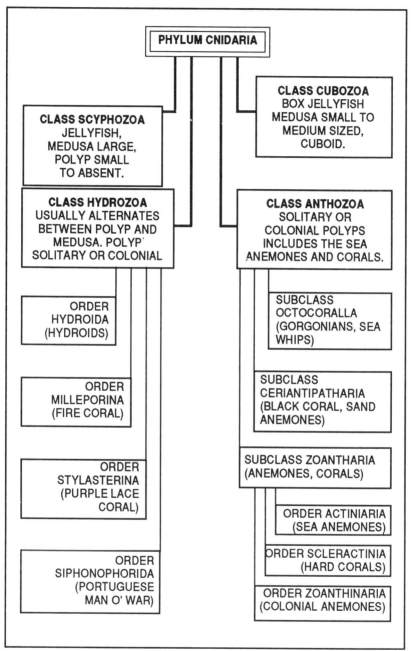

Classification of the cnidarians.

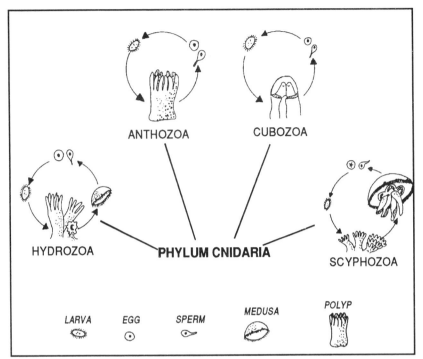

ANTHOZOA

CUBOZOA

HYDROZOA

PHYLUM CNIDARIA

SCYPHOZOA

LARVA EGG SPERM MEDUSA POLYP

Alternation of generations in Cnidaria.

sperm and egg to produce polyps, offspring unlike either parent. Polyps reproduce asexually (without sexual activity), releasing new medusae by "budding."

Conversely, hydrozoans (members of the Class Hydrozoa, like fire coral) live most of their lives as polyps, but reproduce asexually to produce a jellyfish offspring. This jellyfish, in turn, reproduces sexually to form new polyps. The Portuguese Man O' War is a unique hydrozoan because it is a

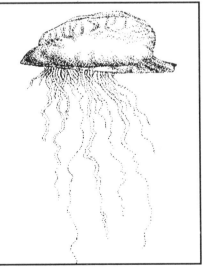

Portuguese Man O' War.

complex colony of polyps suspended from a gas-filled bladder.

Members of the Class Cubozoa are small (1 to 2 inches across the bell) jellyfish common in tropical seas. They have a medusa form and produce new medusae directly from larvae, thus suppressing the polyp body form.

In contrast, the Class Anthozoa, which includes sea anemones, soft corals, and true (stony) corals, has no medusa stage at all. New polyps form directly from fertilized eggs released by the polyps.

Scleractinian Corals

The master builder of the coral reef, the living coral polyp, is a soft-bodied anthozoan that varies in size from the diameter of a pinhead to more than 12 inches across. Scleractinian corals differ from other anthozoans by their ability to secrete a hard calcareous skeleton. It is this capability that makes them the primary builders of the reef's framework.

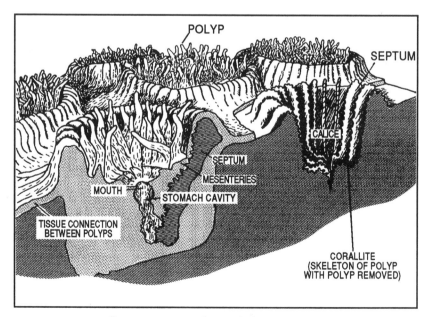

Cross section through living coral.

Their skeleton is formed of minute bundles of microscopic needles of calcium carbonate (aragonite) or *sclerodermites*. The name scleractinian coral refers to the hard rays of which the skeleton is composed.

Study a stony coral! It is covered with thousands of tiny limestone cups. As the coral colony expands and grows upward, polyps divide and extend and enlarge their limy cups. It is within these protective cups that most scleractinian coral polyps remain during daylight.

The individual polyp has a simple body design. Looking

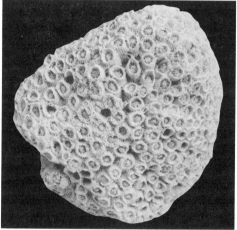

Cavernous star coral skeleton.

very much like a miniature sea anemone, it consists essentially of a fleshy, tube-shaped sack internally partitioned with spoke-like ridges. At the top of the sack is a single opening ringed with stinging tentacles. Through this mouth, food and water are taken in and wastes, sperm, and eggs are expelled. Circlets of six (or multiples of six), smooth tentacles are used to paralyze and capture drifting planktonic animals. The polyp anchors itself to the calcium carbonate cup with a basal disk.

Most corals lead sedentary lives, but a few solitary corals, like the fungus coral, can flip over and scuttle across the sea floor by "walking" on their tentacles.

Many scleractinian corals are colonial, consisting of billions of individual polyps produced by the budding of a single polyp! Although each polyp behaves as an individual, colonial polyps are interconnected by tissue and nerves that extend from one polyp to the next. The distance between polyps may be narrow or wide, or indistinct, as is true with brain corals in which the valleys between ridges are lined with the overlapping tentacles.

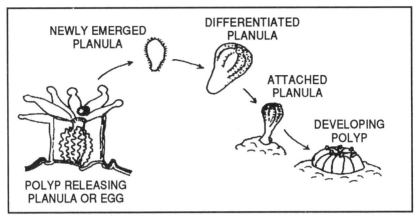

Life cycle of scleractinian coral.

Reproduction

Scleractinian corals reproduce sexually by producing sperm and eggs that combine to produce diminutive coral larvae called planulae. The tiny (less than 0.001 inch long) planula propels itself through the water near the surface with hair-like cilia. The free swimming planula may move through the shallow waters for hours or months in search of a home.

Planulae that survive the multitude of predators swim down to find a suitable substrate on which to grow. Almost immediately the planula flattens out and begins to secrete the limy skeleton that will anchor it to the bottom. In no time at all the planula changes into a polyp and the process of building the colony begins.

Mass-Spawning Event

In the Pacific each year, on a few nights following the full moon in late spring or early summer, hundreds of species of hard corals release eggs and sperm simultaneously. Unlike any other event in the animal kingdom, the synchronized mass-spawning event has the excitement and predictability of a Fourth of July fireworks display.

The spectacular festival of coral reproduction has been observed regularly in Australia, Fiji, and Japan. It occurs just after dark and the great billowing clouds of sperm released into the reef waters have been compared to an upside-down snowstorm. Within hours of release, the eggs are fertilized and millions of these tiny planulae set off in search of a place on which to settle. Hermaphroditic corals (polyps that have both male and female reproductive cells) produce eggs and sperm at different times to prevent self fertilization.

Mass-spawning events have not, as yet, been observed in the Caribbean Sea, the Red Sea, or the waters of Hawaii. Where sexual reproduction has been observed in these areas, eggs are fertilized by sperm inside the polyp. The resulting planulae are then brooded within the polyp, along the swollen edges of mesenterial tissue. A pear-shaped mass of cells is then ejected from the parent coral and begins its quest for a home.

Asexual Reproduction

Once a coral planula attaches to the substrate and forms the polyp, the colony begins to develop by asexual division. New polyps are split from the original polyp by budding and deposit additional skeletal material. Colonial corals, through such asexual multiplication, grow upward and outward to enormous size and age, and produce prodigious quantities of larval progeny.

Two patterns of growth and reproduction have been observed in scleractinian corals: 1) corals that produce large numbers of small adults (the opportunists), and 2) corals that reproduce less often, but exhibit long, slow growth.

Where the available substrate is too hostile for delicate planulae to settle, colonial boulder corals may produce separate polyp "buds" asexually. Clones produced in this manner help to colonize otherwise inhospitable areas and can be formed at any time. Observers in the Pacific report that the brown corals, *Pocillopora* and *Seriatopa*, reproduce asexually through the novel method of polyps "bailing out" (abandoning the parent colony) to begin their *own* colony.

Asexual reproduction also commonly occurs when coral colonies, particularly the branching corals, are broken off by heavy seas. Because they are composed of so many polyps, it is quite easy for the broken colonies to survive. This may, in fact, be the primary way branching corals reproduce.

Juvenile forms of the solitary fungus corals also can reproduce asexually by breaking in half to form two (or more) individual corals.

Zooxanthellae

Reef-building (hermatypic) corals differ from other scleractinians primarily in their ability to secrete massive limy skeletons. The success of these corals is in no small measure related to the symbiotic algae, the zooxanthellae. These zooxanthellae are dinoflagellates of the species, *Zooxanthella microadriaticum.* Well-founded estimates indicate that the plant component in hermatypic corals accounts for nearly as much of the weight as the animal, about 55 percent animal and 45 percent plant.

The mutually beneficial alliance (symbiosis) between the host coral and the zooxanthellae was proven in tests conducted in the 1960s. Hermatypic corals build skeletons three times faster in sunlight than in darkness. What otherwise would be, at best, weak colony development becomes a super coral with zooxanthellae. Planulae of hermatypic corals carry zooxanthellae away from the parent polyp. The zooxanthellae present in any coral colony, accordingly, is host specific.

Zooxanthellae convert energy from sunlight into fuel for their reproduction and nutrition. Within the tissue lining the polyp's stomach, the zooxanthellae cultivate a garden of food supplies. On a sunny day, at least 90 percent of the polyp's daily food requirements will be provided by this source. Nearly 98 percent of the food produced by the zooxanthellae is transferred to the host coral, making the tiny plants a major source of energy for the coral.

By making use of carbon dioxide and other waste products produced by the coral, the zooxanthellae remove materials that would inhibit skeleton formation. In this manner, water chemistry, which would otherwise inhibit skeleton formation (acidity or low pH and organic phosphorous), is suitably modified.

Feeding

Although the food supplied by the zooxanthellae is significant, its manufacture is dependent partially upon nutrients in the food captured by the coral polyps. By day, corals commonly fold their flower-like tentacles and shrink back into protective cups of lime, but at night, the reef comes alive as each polyp blooms and extends its tentacles into lucent waters. Corals are nocturnal feeders, voracious predators feeding on the microscopic animals drifting by on ocean currents.

When the tentacles engage their prey, barbed darts are triggered that inject a venom to paralyze the victim. The stinging mechanism (the nematocysts lining the tentacles and mesenterial filaments) is a highly complex system. A specific vibration range (generated by the movement of a tiny reef animal, for example) triggers a cnidocil on the surface of the cnidoblast, which in turn releases the nematocyst.

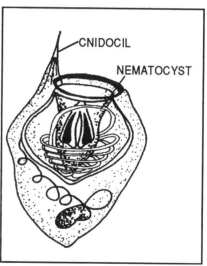

Cross section of cnidoblast.

As the food is captured, it is moved into the polyp's mouth by gentle sweeping movements of the tentacles. A net of mucus can be secreted by the tentacles to help trap and hold prey. Even tiny fish are caught in the tentacles and passed, one to another, down to the mouth. Partial digestion begins in the mesenterial tissues and then, in the polyp's stomach, the food is fully digested. Through the interconnections between polyps, nutrition is provided for the entire colony. Because cnidarians lack complete digestive systems, waste products must be ejected from the polyp's mouth.

Corals are selective predators, eating only bacteria and minute zooplankton (small floating aquatic animals: crustaceans, jellyfish, and various larval forms), small fish, and drifting organic matter. As a rule,

Pillar coral polyps extended during day.

they *do not* feed on algae or other phytoplankton. Corals commonly feed at night, either because zooxanthellae provide adequate food by day or coral predators are less active in the darkness.

Both captured food and nutrition provided by zooxanthellae provide energy and enzymes needed by the coral to grow and secrete calcium carbonate at the base of the polyp. Vertical skeletal supports (septa) are secreted between paired mesenteries like the spokes of a wheel.

Growth

Many corals have common names (staghorn coral, brain coral, plate coral), which often describe their growth form. In many cases, these terms are at least as useful as the Latin or Greek scientific names. The genetic composition of the coral polyp determines the pattern of its skeletal growth, and each coral species can be identified, within certain limits, by its particular growth form.

In addition to genetic controls, the shape corals take is determined by several factors including light and substrate. The abundance of sunlight is determined by depth,

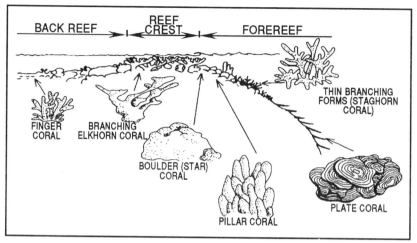

Distribution of coral growth forms.

and in deeper water, corals tend to grow in sheets or plates. Rather than growing upward, new polyps grow along the edges of sheets.

The massive mound-like corals require stability and do best on relatively flat substrate. As new polyps are added between old polyps, a new layer of calcium carbonate is added growing upward over the existing surface of the mound. In fact, these layers provide a history very much like the rings in a cross section of tree trunk. The accumulation of layers of coral growth enables scientists to estimate the age of the coral colony. Branching coral growth is also tree-like as branches grow longer when new polyps are added.

The shapes of other corals result from competition with algal growth and the need to remove sediment, for example, corals with vertical sides, like pillar corals.

Growth rates vary considerably among corals depending on skeletal form. Branching corals are the fastest growing, but they have correspondingly short life expectancies. In contrast, the massive corals are the slowest forms, and they may live hundreds of years.

Studies of aggression among Caribbean corals indicate that some slow-growing corals exhibit aggressive behavior toward the fast-growing branching corals. The aggressive corals fight off and kill the competing corals with their mesenterial filaments. Conversely, other researchers have found evidence that in the Pacific, the fast-growing branching corals may be the more aggressive form.

Growth rates may be slowed by poor environmental conditions or by predators. The coral colony is always under attack by other reef dwellers. Since the reef offers food and shelter to a wide array of mobile animals, it is not surprising that many of these animals prey on small coral polyps. Parrotfish, some damselfish, carnivorous snails, fire worms, and the crown-of-thorns starfish are a few of the more aggressive predators.

The coral colony is always at risk any time the environmental conditions are degraded. In addition to the light and depth, other environmental factors controlling growth rate are salinity, temperature, currents, and clarity. Slowed growth, and resulting bacterial or algal infestations are but a few of the potentially damaging conditions that threaten the reef. Based on percentage of cover, coral framework may not be the dominant reef component, but without it, no coral reef ecosystem can exist.

OTHER FRAMEWORK BUILDERS

The importance of corals as significant reef builders was recognized in the 18th century, but it was 1959 before reef investigators discovered that coral-like algae were responsible for more of the construction on many coral reefs than were the scleractinian corals.

Coralline Algae

With a few notable exceptions, most marine plants are algae. Although many algae are single-celled plants, other algae may resemble higher plants with structures that are similar to roots, stems, and leaves lacking connective tissue. Despite their vast numbers, less than 10 percent of the algae secretes a calcium carbonate skeleton like that formed by scleractinian corals.

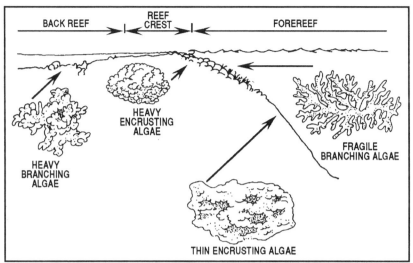

Distribution of coralline algae growth forms.

Most calcareous algae, including the browns, greens, and articulated reds, have skeletons that decompose after death, and, as a result, are not important as framework builders. One type, however, the red encrusting (coralline) algae, can contribute substantially to the reef framework, particularly in cold-water or in high-energy conditions. For example, on shallow, high-energy reefs, red algae such as *Lithothamnion* form a thick crust on all hard surfaces. In deeper or calmer waters, the same red algae sculpt delicate, branching crusts. In waters as deep as 60 feet or more, other red algae (*Peyssonellia*) will form thin crusts. The branching coralline red algae can grow an impressive 0.8 to 1.5 inches each year.

Hydrozoans

Though less important reef builders than scleractinian corals, certain hydrozoans (*Millepora* and *Stylaster*) can add substantially to the reef

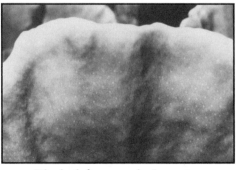

Bladed fire coral, Jamaica.
(Note large and small pores.)

framework. *Millepora*, the fire coral, frequently dominates shallow reefs. It tends to proliferate on dead or damaged reefs as well as those where environmental conditions do not favor healthy corals.

Like scleractinian corals, *Millepora* is host to symbiotic zooxanthellae that live within its inner tissues. It is distinguished from scleractinian corals by its smooth calcareous skeleton. Although it lacks the well-defined cups of stony corals, its surface is dotted with thousands ("mille") of pores through which polyps extend. *Millepora* has 2 very different polyps: The dactylozooids are food-gathering and defensive individuals that live in dactylopores. These are equipped with venomous nematocysts. The gastrozooids are individuals specialized for food intake and digestion, and live in the larger, less numerous gastropores.

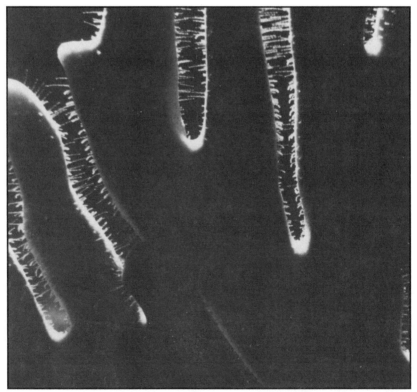

Branching fire coral showing nematocysts.

Millepora is opportunistic as well as prolific. It can grow on almost any substrate in deep or shallow water. It is commonly found growing on man-made objects such as permanent mooring cables and chains, as well as encrusting any number of soft corals.

Like stony corals, the shape assumed by *Millepora* varies with water energy. In shallow, high-energy waters, *Millepora complanata* typically grows upright in flat, box-like plates. It is commonly golden in color and its top edges are tipped in white. In deeper waters, *Millepora alcicornis* commonly forms branches and encrusting shapes that can be flat, round, or conform to the shape of whatever is encrusted.

A far more fragile hydrozoan and much less important reef builder is the delicate lace coral, *Stylaster*. Although it is sometimes found in shallow water shaded from the sunlight and protected from the surge (under overhangs or the lips of boulder corals), it usually resides in deeper waters.

Stylaster has a distinctive lacy fan shape that seldom grows higher than 4 inches. Its coloring ranges from rose through lavender, white and red. It is easily distinguished from stony corals and, for that matter, even other hydrozoans, and unlike other hydrozoans, it has no free-swimming medusae.

Sclerosponges

Deeper on the reef, in darkened caves and tunnels, the primary builders of the reef framework are the hard sponges of the Class Sclerospongiae. These sponges are encased in a hard limy skeleton composed of bundles of calcareous needles, similar to those of the scleractinian corals. Like many common sponges, sclerosponges have silica (glass) spicules. The soft body is similar to other sponges, but forms a thin veneer of soft tissues over the hard skeleton. The sclerosponges typically have a soft orange coloring and their diameters range from 4 inches to nearly 3 feet.

Pink tube sponges, Andros, Bahamas.

CHAPTER 7

CEMENTERS AND BINDERS

The framework created through the diligent work of the coral polyps and their associates, although important, is still only one component of the reef structure. As the remains of coral skeletons and coralline algae are eroded by the sea's endless pounding, they crumble into coral sand. In time, the framework and the sediments are cemented together to form solid reefs of stony coral. The cement binding the skeletal framework and reef debris together is composed of encrusting plants and animals. These organisms function as cementers, binders, bafflers (slowing water currents), and secondary reef framework builders.

CORALLINE ALGAE AND HYDROZOANS

In addition to their role in framework construction, the coralline algae and hydrozoans are important cementers that lay down thick encrusting deposits of lime to help bind the reef. Growth rates as great as 0.6 inch per year have been recorded for encrusting coralline algae in warm water. Although they can live in deeper water, these algae are particularly important in shallow waters where pounding waves would destroy many binders, such as sponges, soft corals, and the mossy bryozoans and other vital encrusting and cementing animals.

SPONGES

Consider the lowly reef sponge. Geologic records indicate that these invertebrate animals have been around for at least 650 million years. Sponges comprise as much as 10 percent of the reef and in lagoonal patch reefs or nutrient-rich waters, the percentage can be much higher. They provide shelter to a broad range of reef animals.

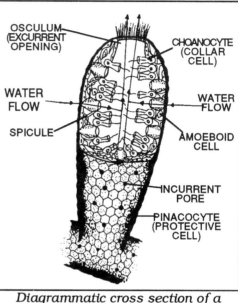

Diagrammatic cross section of a sponge (Phylum Porifera).

Sponges are grouped in the Phylum Porifera, the pore-bearers. They are the least complex of the multicellular organisms, lacking true tissues, organs, or nervous systems. All sponges are sessile animals.

Nevertheless, the fact that sponges have survived millions of years indicates that they are well suited to their tasks. The many specialized cells of the sponge form a sack-like, three-layered body designed for efficient water filtration, feeding, and reproduction.

A simple sponge is basically a hollow vase with three layers: 1) a protective outer skin of tough cells called pinacocytes; 2) an inner lining of choanocytes (flagellated "collar" cells); and 3) a disorganized mass of amoeba-like cells separating the outer and inner layers. These amoeboid cells transport food and waste products, repair damaged cells, and form microscopic needle-like spicules. These branching skeletal elements provide the supporting framework for most sponges.

An Amazing Filter

The collar cells' function is to provide for water movement, feeding, and respiration of the colony. (At this level of organization, it is impossible to distinguish solitary individuals from colonial animals.) Sponges feed by filtering plankton and other floating material (including coral mucus, detritus, and cyanobacteria) from the reef waters.

Water enters the body cavity of the sponge through numerous "dermal" pores in the sponge walls. Then the whipping movement of tiny flagella on the collar cells creates a current inside the sponge. As the water passes these cells, oxygen and food particles are effectively filtered and captured by the collar cells and the strained water is pumped out through the large opening (osculum) at the top of the sponge.

Unlike scleractinian corals, sponges can thrive in turbid water and, as a result, often dominate lagoonal reef communities. Reef scientists have observed that a typical Jamaican reef supports a sponge population large enough to filter the entire water column every 24 hours.

The Shape of Sponges

Although there are simple vase-shaped sponges, the coral reef is festooned with a rich profusion of multi-colored shapes. Sponges shaped like tubes, fingers, pipes, baskets, vases and bowls are everywhere. Not all sponges have a distinctive shape. In some zones, the substrate is blanketed with a shapeless mass of sheet-like sponge growth.

Grey pineapple sponge, Jamaica.

Explosions of color radiate from sponges even in deep water, where sunlight is attenuated. Lavender, gold, vermilion, pink, and yellow are but a few of the colors exhibited by reef sponges. Because of their variable colors and shapes, sponges are classified only by the form and composition of their skeletal elements.

Sponge Classes

Nearly all reef sponges (approximately 95 percent) belong to the Class Demospongiae, having skeletons made primarily of interlacing organic fibers called spongin. The remaining 5 percent belongs to the Class Calcarea, including those sponges with spicules formed of calcium carbonate, and the Class Sclerospongiae having silicious spicules embedded in a hard calcareous skeleton. The Class Hexactinellidae, lacking an outer cell layer and having mineralized spicules composed of glass-like silica is absent from reef areas.

Sponge Reproduction

Sponges reproduce sexually by releasing sperm during a phenomenon called "smoking." In the precisely timed event, male sponges eject a "smoke" of sperm into the water around the reef, while at the same time, female sponges emit a string of eggs. Eventually, the eggs may be fertilized and develop into free-swimming larvae that then settle onto suitable hard surfaces and grow into sponges. Sponges also can reproduce asexually by budding.

Sponge Hotel

Sponges have few natural enemies, which accounts for the extraordinary potpourri of organisms living on or in them. Some sponges have a symbiotic relationship with minute zoanthids (colonial anemones) or cyanobacteria living on their surfaces. Others have internal parasites such as the tiny white worm, *Syllis spongia*, which thrives in the touch-me-not sponge. A broad range of symbionts and parasites (zooxanthellae, shrimps, crabs, and brittle stars are but a few) find safety and abundant food within the sponge's protection and hospitality.

Friend or Foe

Some sponge species, such as the red-brown encrusting sponge (*Hemectyon ferox*), kill corals by overgrowing and shading them. Still others produce mucus-secreting larvae that destroy coral polyps, and many sponges bore deeply into the coral substrate for protection. Often the whole underside of an otherwise healthy coral reef is completely undermined and weakened by boring sponges such as the yellow boring sponge (*Cliona*), and eventually storms combine with violent wave action to break down these reef areas.

Other sponges, like the orange and gray encrusting sponge (*Mycale laevis*), actually reinforce the lower, dead surfaces of coral plates and cement the coral sediment together into coral rock. These sponges assist other cementing organisms such as the soft corals in forming a new substrate for another generation of coral reef.

SOFT CORALS

Carpet anemone, Jamaica.

Soft corals take a variety of forms (whip corals, black corals, sea feathers, sea fans, and sea pens), all of which belong to the Class Anthozoa, which also includes hard corals and anemones. Other bottom-stabilizing anthozoans include the sea anemones (Actinaria), the colonial anemones (Zoanthidia), and the stony corals (Scleractinia).

It would be a mistake to regard the lesser known relatives of the stony corals as unimportant. There are reef communities along the Great Barrier Reef, for example, where soft corals represent more than 50 percent of the living tissue on the surface of the reef.

The most diverse cementers belong to the Subclass Alcyonaria, including the sea pens (Order Pennatulacea) and the sea fans, sea feathers, and flexible whip corals (Order Gorgonacea). These soft corals lack the rigid skeletons of hard corals and are supported instead by a flexible rod of the protein, gorgonin. Covering the core of gorgonin is a veneer of calcareous spicules.

Close-up of sea feather, showing polyps.

The large colonies of fleshy polyps have sack-like bodies and eight fringed (pinnate) tentacles, unlike the stony corals that have six (or multiples of six) smooth tentacles. Like many other cnidarians, some of these marine animals have symbiotic algae living within their tissues that provide daytime nutrition by converting sunlight into food.

In the Subclass Ceriantipatharia, includes the sand anemones (Ceriantharia), which form a mucus tube, and the black corals (Antipatharia), which have a skeleton of horny material.

Soft corals would seem to be at the mercy of an endless stream of predators and yet, with the notable exception of the beautiful flamingo tongue snail and the equally beautiful nudibranchs, these corals appear to have few natural enemies. Poisonous chemicals in their tissues give soft corals a foul taste, and less discriminating would-be predators are further dissuaded by the needle-like spicules that protect the polyp's fleshy tissue.

Soft corals reproduce and grow rapidly and might conceivably overgrow the hard corals of the reef were it not for their fragile nature. Violent wave action during tropical storms inflicts severe damage on soft corals with a correspondingly high mortality.

BRYOZOANS

Among the earliest stabilizers of uninhabited substrate are delicate little plant-like animals belonging to the **Phylum Bryozoa**. As the very name suggests ("bryo" means moss, "zoan" means animal), the colony resembles moss. For this reason, bryozoans go largely unnoticed in the reef environment.

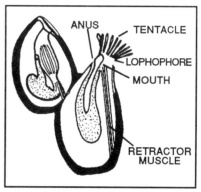

Bryozoan anatomy.

Bryozoans are colonial and commonly may be found growing under large plate corals or in darkened crevices at all depths. There they are free to compete for food and space with algae and sponges and can escape predators.

Moss animals may be free-standing and branching in shape such as *Bugula*, or they may form flat calcareous or organic crusts such as *Membranipora*. Each animal (zooid) in the colony has an external shell into which it can retract for protection.

Bryozoans feed by filtering plankton with a ring of tentacles called the lophophore. These ciliated tentacles are retracted through contractile muscles activated by nerve impulses.

Individuals within the colony have specialized functions, including sexual reproduction and larval brooding, as well as providing protection from predators or sediments. Among the typical predators are parrotfish, sea urchins, chitons, sea spiders, and nudibranchs. On the Great Barrier Reef alone, there are estimated to be over 300 species of resident bryozoans.

LESSER CEMENTERS

There are numerous other small animals that help to bind the reef elements together. Among the minute creatures that cement their skeletons to the reef are the polychaete tube worms, oysters, attached snails, and some of the single-celled foraminifera. Typically, these animals contribute little to the stabilization of the reef framework except when they are present in enormous numbers.

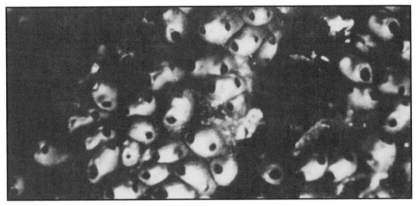

Encrusting bryozoan, Belize.

Serpulid worms encrusting red fan sponge.

CHAPTER 8

REEF ASSOCIATES I

FLOATERS, SWIMMERS, IMMOBILE BOTTOM DWELLERS

The coral reef exists as nature's most distinct domain of life, as different from other regions of the ocean as it is from land. Differentiated by the uniqueness of its population as well as its environment, it attracts a diversity of reef life because it offers living spaces, variety of food, and safe spawning grounds for breeding aggregations.

Many plants and animals that play no active role in building or cementing the reef structure live around and within the reef. It is not unusual for reef associates to

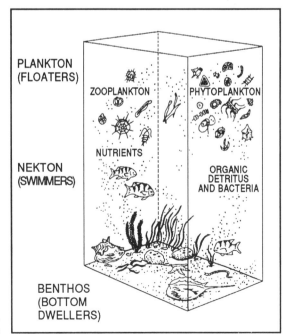

Distribution of marine organisms.

outnumber framework and cementing organisms by 10 to 1. These associates include both unattached plants and animals that move freely along the bottom or drift through the water, as well as many plants and some animals that are permanently attached to the hard surface of the reef.

Reef associates may be described, in terms of their function on the reef, as primary producers or consumers. Because of the diversity of life styles exhibited by consumers, they may be further divided into: 1) plankton, which float or swim so weakly that they are at the mercy of water currents; 2) nekton, which swim freely through the water; and 3) benthos, which live on or within the substrate.

PRIMARY PRODUCERS

Primary producers are those organisms capable of producing their own food by photosynthesis or chemosynthesis. Primary producers in reef areas include phytoplankton, cyanobacteria, benthic algae, and higher plants including sea grasses.

Phytoplankton

The oceans of the world teem with microscopic marine plants called phytoplankton. Too small to be seen by the unaided eye, these countless floating algae and cyanobacteria are regarded as the sea's invisible food supply. Although they are microscopic, these organisms form the base of the ocean food web, and nearly all life in the sea from the smallest one-celled animal to the greatest whale ultimately owes its survival to phytoplankton.

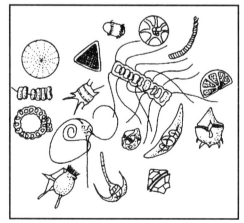

Phytoplankton.

Since these photosynthetic algae and blue-green bacteria derive their energy from the sun, their movements are commonly restricted to ocean depths less than 300 feet.

Misconceptions

Because clear reef waters typically have low-nutrient levels and correspondingly little phytoplankton, it was generally held that coral reefs were oceanic zones of high consumption and low primary production. Nothing could be farther from the truth. Although the ocean contains phytoplankton that can be measured in breath-taking tonnage, the warm reef waters are low in nutrients and host a multiplicity of primary producers that are reshaping old beliefs by being extremely efficient recyclers.

Much of the primary productivity of coral reefs is related to symbiotic algae and bacteria living among the reef organisms in mutualistic relationships in which both symbionts enjoy the benefits. Symbiotic zooxanthellae and cyanobacteria live not only in the tissues of corals, but have also been discovered living in the tissues of giant clams, sponges, and even in the cytoplasm of single-celled animals (foraminifera). Sev-

Upside-down jellyfish, Maldives.

eral jellyfish have been found to contain symbiotic zooxanthellae as well, including the beautiful *Cassiopeia*, the upside-down jellyfish that is often seen gently pulsating, upside down on the bottom, sunning its zooxanthellae.

Benthic Algae and Bacteria

Benthic (bottom-dwelling) algae and bacteria are particularly important to the reef community, where they form underwater pastures for a multitude of fish, sea urchins, and many other herbivores. Perhaps the activity of the three-spot damselfish best demonstrates the importance of algae on the reef. These damselfish actively cultivate "farms" of filamentous algae by nipping off the buds of staghorn corals to encourage the algal growth. Each fish then defines the perimeter of its farm, which it fearlessly defends against all intruders.

Algae are classified by the pigments used in the process of photosynthesis. The common names of algae reflect the striking range of pigment colors, including golden algae (Division Chrysophyta), green algae (Division Chlorophyta), brown algae (Division Phaeophyta), and red algae (Division Rhodophyta). Many algae bear a superficial resemblance to higher plants, but are easily distinguished by their lack of true leaves, stems, and roots with conducting tissue.

The most significant of the attached primary producers on the shallow reefs are the red, green, and brown fleshy algae. These algae are always present on reefs, but they increase in abundance when nutrient supplies increase and when grazers are lost, whether by fishing, collecting, or dieoff.

Another important producer is the blue-green filamentous bacterium (cyanobacterium) commonly found with golden algae. Although cyanobacteria can photosynthesize and were formerly called blue-green algae, they have primitive cells lacking a nucleus and are not true algae. Most cyanobacteria form surface mats, but some filamentous algae, such as green algae, have been observed boring into the skeletons of scleractinian corals.

Some algae even secrete calcareous skeletons much like those of the stony corals. The most common of these forms are the coralline red algae, which are important framework builders and cementers.

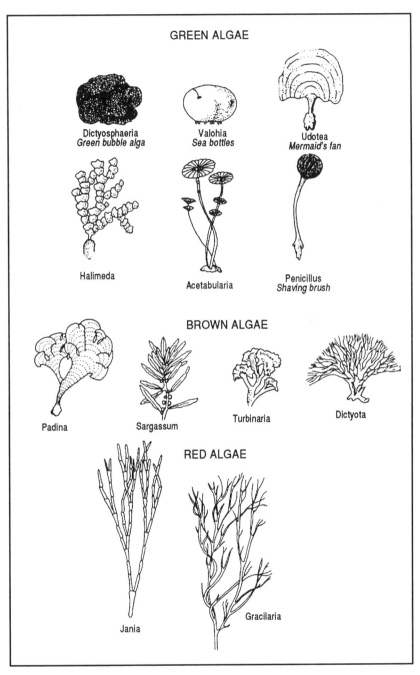

Common reef algae.

Other red algae have segmented or articulated calcareous skeletons, as do many green and a few brown algae. Most of the shallow-reef sediments are formed from broken skeletons of these calcareous algae, which commonly include species of *Halimeda* and *Penicillus* (green algae), *Amphiroa* and *Jania* (red algae), and *Padina* (brown alga).

Higher Plants

There are few true marine seed-bearing plants. By far the most common is *Thalassia testudinum*, the turtle grass. Much less abundant are other species of grasses, including *Syringodium* (manatee grass) and *Halodule* (shoal grass). Such higher plants form thick grassy meadows that baffle ocean currents, filter nutrients and sediments from the water and bind sediments together to form shallow banks.

The sandy or muddy banks not only help prevent erosion, but also provide a nursery ground, a protected area filled with nutrients, for a wide range of life. The young of many animals including turtles, sea horses, sea urchins, clams, snails, sea hares, and a multitude of juvenile fish thrive in seagrass meadows. Many biologists believe that grass beds play a significant role in the importation of nutrients to the reef by fish. Fish who have been grazing on grass beds have been observed defecating on the reef, thereby placing nutrients directly on reef organisms.

Mangrove Swamps

Mangrove trees grow in the coastal areas where mud and sand accumulate. Mangroves put down roots in disorganized tangles and anchor to the boggy, salty sediment. The roots rise stilt-like above the water and intertwine with

Black mangrove at low tide, Andros, Bahamas. (Note roots.)

those of other trees, forming a natural net to trap pollutants, debris, and sediment that would inhibit reef growth. Thus, although it is unlikely that a coral reef would form in a mangrove swamp, coastal mangroves are important filters that are vital to the reef's continued good health. In fact, it is estimated that mangroves once lined 70 percent of the world's tropical and subtropical coastlines.

DRIFTERS

What more apt name for a group of marine organisms that is so broadly distributed in every part of the world's oceans? The very word plankton is derived from the Greek word for wanderer. Virtually all the life adrift, afloat, or swimming feebly in the ocean is considered to be planktonic, and these organisms are a major food source for the animals that construct and live in the reef community.

Generally, plankton are divided into two categories: phytoplankton and zooplankton. Phytoplankton are those organisms that can synthesize their own food by photosyn-

thesis using sunlight or chemosynthesis. The other plankton members include the vast menagerie of drifting animals called zooplankton. Almost every phylum of marine animal can be found in zooplankton. Although they spend most of their life as bottom dwellers, many ma-

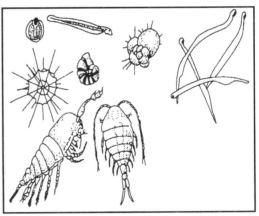

Zooplankton.

rine animals living on the reef have floating larval or juvenile stages that are important food sources for still other reef animals. Two major groups of animals spend their adult lives as drifters: jellyfish and their relatives, and copepods.

Jellyfish, Cubomedusae, and Comb Jellies

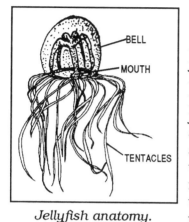

Jellyfish anatomy.

Members of the Phylum Cnidaria that spend most of their adult lives as floating medusa or jellyfish belong to the Class Scyphozoa. Although they have primitive nerves and muscles, jellyfish are at the mercy of wind and water currents and are among the largest members of the marine plankton. They vary in size from almost microscopic to several feet in diameter and their tentacles may extend 40 feet or more below the "bell" or main body of the jellyfish. Nematocysts are concentrated in the tentacles and are used for feeding or defense.

Members of the Class Cubozoa (Order Cubomedusae) resemble small scyphozoan jellyfish except that they have 4 tentacles or groups of tentacles. "Cubos" or "sea wasps" are noted for delivering painful, venomous stings to divers and swimmers. They commonly live in deep water during the day and rise to the surface at night.

Unlike the cnidarian medusa, which swims by pulsating its bell, the comb jelly, of the Phylum Ctenophora, moves by using eight rows of cilia on the outside of its transparent body. Although similar to jellyfish, comb jellies lack stinging nematocysts. In addition, the comb jellies, unlike the Cnidaria, have a com-

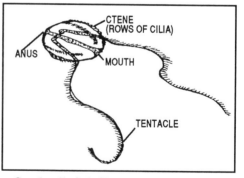

Comb jellyfish (Ctenophore anatomy).

plete digestive system with a separate opening for waste removal. They may be bioluminescent and can be seen near the surface at night.

Copepods

Copepods are microscopic, cylindrical or pear-shaped arthropods with oar-shaped appendages. Most are regarded as planktonic, because they swim too weakly to control their direction. Others are benthonic and a few are parasitic. Although less than 1/8 inch long, planktonic copepods are abundant in marine waters and form an important food source for many reef animals.

SWIMMERS

Visitors to a coral reef are amazed by the profusion of life that abounds there. Surrounding the reef is the vast emptiness of the open ocean, but on the reef, in its shallow lagoons and its coral gardens, there lives the greatest diversity of swimmers (nekton) that can be found in any of the world's oceans. These swimmers do not just include fish, but also marine reptiles, marine mammals, and the "jet-propelled" cephalopods.

Cephalopods

The cuttlefish, squid, octopus, and chambered nautilus are relatives of the clams and snails that move through the water using jet propulsion. No other member of the Phylum Mollusca demonstrates so clearly the adaptability of animals to a changing life style as do the members of the Class Cephalopoda. Their bodies have been modified for efficient movement through the water, and they have

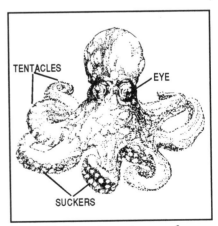

External anatomy of an octopus.

evolved extremely well-developed vision and touch for active lives as swimming predators.

The very name "cephalopod" (cephalon = head, pod = foot) refers to the modification of the foot into a ring of prehensile tentacles around the head. The tentacles are lined with powerful suckers for grasping and holding prey (or mate while mating) and crawling over the bottom. In addition, cephalopods have developed powerful beaks for killing prey, breaking shells, and chewing. Their eyes are as well developed as those of mammals and their vision is excellent, making them effective predators.

The members of this class also are among the best swimmers of the invertebrates. To aid in swimming, most cephalopods have either no shell at all or have a thin internal shell, resulting in more flexibility of movement. Squid and cuttlefish, for example, have reduced and internalized their shells, but the chambered nautilus has coiled its chambered external shell and reduced its thickness. Movement is accomplished by drawing water in and forcing it out the funnel, a tube-like extension of the mantle. The squid is among the fastest creatures in the sea.

The swimming ability of the squid is necessary to escape predators, because they are an important food source for many marine creatures, not the least of which are the sperm whales. It is interesting to note that the adult

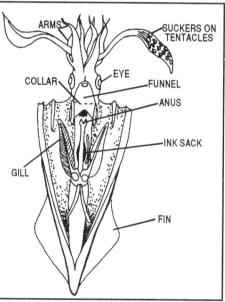

Squid anatomy.

giant squid has been known to grow to a length of 60 feet, which makes it the largest living invertebrate on Earth.

In addition to speed, the cephalopods have other means to escape. If disturbed, all cephalopods can spray a smoke screen of dark ink, then use their speed to escape. Octopus and cuttlefish are truly masters of disguise. By almost instantaneous shifting of pigments in their chromatophores (pigment-carrying cells), they can make rapid color changes to match any background.

Cephalopods are primarily nocturnal. Although daylight sightings are unusual, encounters under the cover of darkness are common. This is also true for many larger predators.

Higher Vertebrates

Porpoises, sea turtles, and sea snakes are commonly seen in reef areas in search of food. In addition, manatee and dugong sightings are not unusual in the grass beds adjacent to coral reefs.

Fish

In a world where little fish feed bigger fish that feed even bigger fish, it is on the shallow-reef crest and seaward on the deep reef where thousands of fish school in a profusion of life that staggers the imagination. Imagine a coral reef, perhaps 100 acres in area. It would not be unusual to find that it shelters and supports more than 500 species of fish. This incredibly diverse fauna can range from the tiniest goby 1/2 inch long to whale sharks 50 feet long.

Living Space

Coral reefs do far more than provide a riotous profusion of color and exquisite branching trees and flowers. On the reef there is no wasted space; the tiniest crevice provides safe haven for tenants. Under their sunlit gardens, there lies a darkened labyrinth of intricate tunnels, caves, and narrow passageways, all of which provide cover and concealment to shelter numerous fish.

Reef dwellers have their subdivisions just as humans have theirs. Many reef fish spend only a part of the day or night on the reef. Others may reside within the reef community during a particular season or period in their life cycle; but every neighborhood in the reef community has its unique and proprietary residents.

Grey angelfish.

Many reef fish stake out an area and protect it aggressively. Such *territoriality* is typically determined not by the size of the fish, but by the level of feisty spirit it exhibits. The most pugnacious fish on the whole reef, the three-spot damselfish, is less than 6 inches long!

Multitudes of yellowtail and grunt sway endlessly with the surge above the reef. Enormous barracuda, grouper, and jewfish swim cautiously in the open waters beyond the seaward ramparts. Angelfish peer out of algae-covered caves in coral recesses, and Pacific razorfish lurk within the spines of long-spined urchins. The remarkable flounder with its migrating eye, gobies, blennies, and the burrowing garden eels reside in the sand flats. Tuna, sailfish, marlin and other pelagic visitors from the open sea occasionally cruise the reef.

Schooling

Reef fish that are constantly under the threat of predation tend to school for mutual protection. Schooling fish orient themselves so that the entire school has a field of view of 360°.

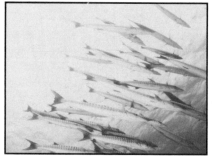

School of barracuda.

When threatened, fish nearest the approaching threat exude a chemical substance, an alarm pheromone perhaps, which alerts other fish. They then close ranks and either attempt to escape or turn, as one, to face the menace. Predators commonly hunt and feed by culling out the weak and are often thwarted by successful schooling.

Feeding

The feeding habits of fish populations are as diverse as the fish themselves. Some subsist as vegetarians. These are herbivores, which are typically small and delicate, such as tangs and damselfish. The parrotfish with its strong, fused teeth is a bit less delicate, but it is an herbivore nonetheless. Although it appears to be eating the coral polyp and skeleton, the parrotfish is actually grazing on boring algae within the coral skeleton. It is estimated in its quest for this tasty algal growth, an average population of parrotfish will crunch, swallow, and dump on the reef as much as 1/2 a ton of digested coral sand in a single year.

The carnivores are widely varied in their selection of foods. The big predators - many sharks, barracuda, jacks, groupers, and moray eels - have voracious appetites and eat large reef fish. Smaller carnivores like the trumpetfish and scorpionfish hunt and eat correspondingly smaller prey. Squirrelfish and wrasses eat shrimp and other tiny crustaceans, but interestingly, they are non-competitive since wrasses feed by day and squirrelfish feed at night. Triggerfish, pufferfish, and some wrasses feed on sea urchins, snails, and nudibranchs. Still others eat crustaceans. Some damselfish and triggerfish prefer the mucus of corals, while others, such as filefish, graze on coral polyps. The long-nosed butterfly fish pokes its tube-like snout into coral cracks, like an anteater, in its quest for the tasty little shrimp it prizes.

Some fish are omnivorous and feed on any target of opportunity, plant or animal. Others are more selective and are bottom feeders. These include goatfish, trunkfish and rays, which spend their feeding time foraging through the bottom sediment.

Planktivores strain plankton from the water. During daylight, chromis and silversides siphon plankton from the reef waters, whereas conversely, at night soldierfish feed on the plankton. Among the cleaners (those fish that pick and feed upon parasites from other animals) are gobies, wrasses, and jewel-like fairy basslets.

Manta ray — a planktivore.

Reproduction

Juvenile mortality among reef fish is necessarily high. With a single spawning season commonly producing millions of fertilized eggs, the reef would quickly be overrun with fish it could in no way support, but only two fertilized eggs need to reach maturity to replace their parents and maintain the biological balance.

Reef fish reproduce in a variety of ways. The three-spot damselfish breeds solitarily, gluing its eggs to the coral and guarding them aggressively.

Soldierfish, on the other hand, form breeding aggregations that school to facilitate reproduction and decrease the risk of predation. Although some reef fish bear their offspring live, most reproduce through the simultaneous release of eggs and sperm into the water column.

Spawning rituals produce carefully coordinated clouds of eggs and sperm, or perhaps are stimulated by the female's release of a pheromone similar to the substance a queen bee secretes to entice mates. Floating eggs may travel great distances and, if they survive predation, colonize other reefs. Fertilized eggs commonly develop into planktonic larvae that float freely around the reef community. Still other eggs sink almost immediately. Most juvenile fish find shelter in dark, irregular coral crevices or remain concealed in grass beds until they grow to adulthood.

Adaptations

Nowhere in nature has the art of camouflage been more highly developed than in the enchanted gardens of the coral reef. Scorpionfish, stonefish, and frogfish blend in perfectly against the stony corals surrounding them. Groupers and flounders change colors and shadings as they swim from one multi-colored background to the next.

Many fish are conspicuous in their brilliant colors and distinctive markings. Strange markings and bright colors simplify recognition among members of the same species and perhaps among would-be predators as well. Other markings break up the brilliant colors and often confuse attackers in the sun-dappled water. The four-eyed butterfly fish, for example, has a false eye on its tail that decoys confused predators.

Size is still another factor that determines if a fish will survive in the reef community. One of the tiniest vertebrates in nature's realm, the goby, survives quite nicely by squatting unobtrusively in a sponge. Conversely, the enormous size of the visiting whale shark keeps it safe from most predators, and there are those who protect themselves by using their venomous spines.

Clinging capriciously to coral cliffs are reef fish equipped with a virulent venom and the needle-sharp spines with which to inject it. Among these really passive creatures are the scorpionfish, stonefish, stingray, and the lionfish. Although the spines of all of these may cause a temporary paralysis - and at the very least, severe localized pain - these fish are totally nonaggressive and pose little threat to the alert diver.

Close Friends and Partnerships

Perhaps of all the fascinating and close relationships reef fish may develop with other creatures, none is as peculiar as that of *Carapus*, the pearl fish, that resides inside the body of the five-toothed sea cucumber. It ventures out under cover of darkness to feed, returning at

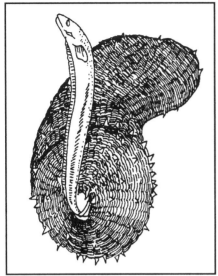

*Pearl fish with
sea cucumber host.*

daybreak to enter backwards through the anus of the sea cucumber.

Among other incredible partnerships is the relationship of the hyperactive Indo-Pacific clownfish and the stinging tentacles of the anemone it swims to when threatened. Another fascinating partner of the anemone is the inconsequential decorator crab. The crab is sheltered and hidden by the anemone and repays the kindness by providing transportation and food for its host.

The relationship between the little cleaner wrasse and large carnivorous reef fish also has been well documented. At numerous underwater grooming stations, these tiny cleaners peck away at troublesome parasites and particles of undigested food on the scales, gills, and teeth of client fish.

ASSOCIATES THAT ATTACH
TO THE BOTTOM

For all the hundreds of creatures that move freely about the reef, there are probably thousands of lesser animals (including barnacles, oysters, and tube worms) that grow to maturity permanently attached to the bottom. There are an estimated 150,000 benthic marine species to be found attached to substrates and at varying depths. Unlike the motile organisms (crabs, snails, starfish, and others) that are able to forage and hunt for prey, attached animals wait for their food to come to them. They can be found on hard rock, firm sediments, soft mud, and sand or burrowed and bored into these substrates. On these permanent moorings, they feed, rest, hide, and flourish.

Brachiopods

Members of the Phylum Brachiopoda, the lamp shells, resemble clams to which they are totally unrelated. A half

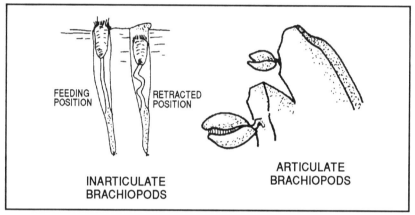

Brachiopod modes of attachment.

billion years ago, this benthic creature was among the most numerous of animals on this planet. In fact, the ducksbill brachiopod (Genus *Lingula*) is the oldest known animal genus, and it has survived the ages, according to the geologic record, virtually without change. *Lingula* lives in a U-shaped, vertical burrow that it excavates in a sandy substrate with its pedicle, a long, muscular stalk.

Other lamp shells attach to rocky substrates with a shorter pedicle. Their favorite spots are typically under boulder corals or coral overhangs in deeper water. Enclosed between the brachiopod's shells are two coiled tentacles forming a ciliated lophophore used for filter feeding. This structure is similar to that used by the bryozoans and horseshoe worms and is used for capturing fine organic particles from the water.

Marine Worms

The sea floor seems to be covered with various types of marine worms. A few of these worms secrete calcareous tubes and are modest reef builders, but most are organic-tube dwellers or those able to move slowly over the reef.

Sabellid polychaete worms.

Polychaetes

Of all the invertebrates on the reef, none are more beautiful than the elegant segmented worms of the Phylum Annelida, Class Polychaeta. The name is derived from "poly" meaning many and "chaeta" meaning bristles. Some poly-chaetes are sessile, others are free swimmers or crawlers. The so-called "sedentary" polychaetes live in burrows or calcareous or organic tubes

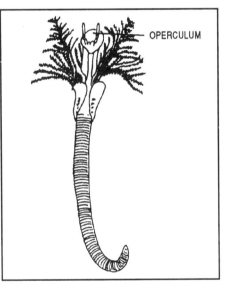

Serpulid Worm.

within the stony coral framework. The errant polychaetes, on the other hand, are voracious predators, which move about in constant search of food.

Feather-duster worms and star and feathered Christmas tree worms belong to the Family Serpulidae. Many serpulids, as well as unsegmented peanut worms (of the Phylum Sipuncula), are effective bioeroders and bore into boulder corals, but they also are prolific enough to build small reefs by secreting calcareous tubes that attach to those of other serpulids or other hard surfaces. The names given to these worms spring from the flamboyance and shape of their ciliated tentacles. When feeding, the tentacles are extended and cilia sweep water toward the mouth and filter out food particles. If threatened, the worm retracts the tentacles into the tube and an operculum (trap door) snaps shut over the tube's opening.

The magnificent fan worms of the Family Sabellidae live in tubes commonly found attached to boulder corals or rooted in soft substrates. These worms are common on all tropical reefs. The tubes are not calcareous, but are composed of tough organic material. The sabellid worm feeds by extending ciliated tentacles and filtering plankton from the water in the same manner as other sedentary worms.

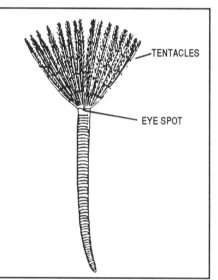

Sabellid worm.

Phoronid Worms

Another group of tube-dwelling worms (Phylum Phoronidea) is more closely related to brachiopods and bryozoans than to the other tube worms. These horseshoe worms resemble, externally, the serpulid feather-duster worms. Unlike the serpulids, however, they trap their food with ciliated tentacles attached to a horseshoe-shaped, or bilobed, lophophore. Because they have a larval form that is identical to brachiopods and bryozoans, phoronids are believed to share a common ancestor with these groups.

Marine worms serve the reef in many important ways. Some worms, like the serpulids, help reinforce the reef structure. Others bore into substrate and constantly undermine the reef. In this way, the corals are being continuously eroded and nutrients are being recycled, maintaining the crucial balance between reef growth and destruction.

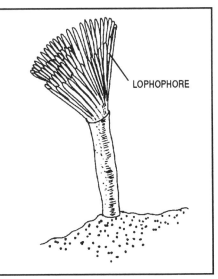

Phoronid worm.

Crustaceans

As numerous as marine worms are, they cannot begin to compare with the number of different marine animals belonging to the Class Crustacea. The very name was meant originally to designate animals having a flexible armor-like "crust." This exoskeleton protects the soft-bodied animals from predation. Among crustaceans highly prized as human food are the prawns, lobsters, shrimp, and crabs.

Crustaceans belong to the world's biggest phylum, the Arthropoda. Members of the phylum are distinguished by their jointed appendages, which may include antennae, claws, and specialized appendages for swimming, walking or eating. Marine arthropods breathe with gills carried on swimming or walking appendages. Arthropods typically grow in quick spurts, throwing off the outgrown exoskeleton (molting) and growing another. Most marine crustaceans are mobile, but one of the most unusual is the highly modified barnacle.

Barnacles

Although commonly found in shallow rocky zones where planktonic food is abundant, barnacles are poorly represented on coral reefs. They belong to the Subclass Cirripedia, and although they bear little resemblance externally to the shrimp or other crustaceans, the animal that lives *inside* the thick calcareous shell does resemble a small shrimp.

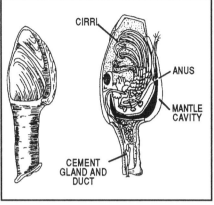

Barnacle anatomy.

The adult barnacle attaches firmly to the substrate (whatever it may be) with a gummy adhesive secreted from glands in its antennae. Being a sessile crustacean, the barnacle commonly lives attached to hard substrates (piers, rocks, oysters, and dock pilings), but its larvae are pelagic and frequently fasten to drifting flotsam as well as migrant turtles, whales, sharks, and other marine animals.

Mollusks

The Phylum Mollusca is the second largest group of invertebrates. Like the arthropods, most marine mollusks are mobile. In addition to the cephalopods, the phylum includes the conchs, chitons, snails, sea hares, nudibranchs, clams, oysters, scallops, tusk shells and many other benthic animals. So numerous are they, that nearly 4,000 species have been catalogued on the Great Barrier Reef alone. The shells of dead mollusks represent a sizeable percentage of the substrate on which new coral reefs develop. Many mollusks have big, fleshy bodies and are harvested as an important food source for humans. The very name, Mollusca, means "soft body."

Most mollusks secrete hard calcareous shells into which they retract when threatened. Although attached mollusks include the jewelbox oyster, razor clams, and vermetid snails, as well as the legendary giant clams; most mollusks have a muscular foot with which they slowly crawl across the sea floor.

The awesome giant clam of the Pacific, *Tridacna gigas*, is threatened with extinction and may soon disappear from the ocean. Heavy predation by commercial and amateur collectors, as well as the impact of pollution (*Tridacna* accumulates heavy metals in its kidneys), bodes badly for this magnificent mollusk. Permitted to live, it grows to impressive proportions, easily 100 pounds in 20 years. Its tremendous size has been attributed to the presence of zooxanthellae in the soft tissue or mantle lining its shells. No one who has ever snorkeled over a giant clam could forget the iridescence and shimmering brilliance of its mantle. Zooxanthellae have also been reported in tunicates.

Ascidians (Tunicates)

Less obvious than the giant clam are the small tunicates. These animals are effective filter feeders that strain organisms and detritus from reef waters. Many biologists believe that tunicates not only keep reef waters clean, but also, through their constant filtering, concentrate nutrients for other marine animals. They are often found in dense colonies attached to the underside of reef caves, ledges, and rocky outcrops, but also can occur as solitary and grouped individuals. Some even have algal symbionts.

The tunicate is sometimes called a "sea squirt" because of its habit of contracting its body when disturbed and squirting water out of its body in two jets. It is a colorful translucent animal having the shape of a miniature vase with an opening at the top for drawing in water and another opening for expelling the water after it has extracted the food and oxygen it requires.

It has been suggested that tunicates bridge the gap between vertebrates and invertebrates. Most marine vertebrates are swimmers as adults. Though a few tunicates are free swimmers throughout their lives, most become

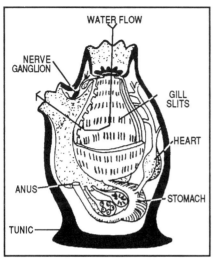

NERVE GANGLION

WATER FLOW

GILL SLITS

HEART

ANUS

STOMACH

TUNIC

Tunicate anatomy.

sessile with maturity and are permanently anchored to the bottom.

They exhibit characteristics of higher animals such as sharks and rays, but appear more closely related to the sponge. There is little about the adult tunicate to associate it with other members of the Phylum Chordata, a group containing humans, mammals, fish, and all other vertebrates. Tunicates belong to the Class Ascidiacea, a group of animals having gill slits and a stiffened rod (notochord), a forerunner of the backbone. However, in its free-swimming larval stage, it looks like a tadpole.

In addition to the variety of life attached to the reef and swimming or floating around the reef, many reef dwellers move quietly along the sea floor. These transient reef inhabitants, which may move about in search of food or space, are as important to the reef as the permanent reef dwellers.

Pencil coral at Columbus Park patch reef, Jamaica.

PLATE I: CARIBBEAN SCLERACTINIAN CORALS (p. 113)

1. Elkhorn coral (*Acropora palmata*); reef crest (5 to 10 feet); Andros, Bahamas.

2. Staghorn coral (*Acropora cervicornis*) and pencil coral (*Madracis mirabilis*); forereef terrace (45 to 50 feet); Discovery Bay, Jamaica.

3. Mounding star coral (*Montastrea annularis*); lower forereef terrace (60 to 70 feet); Andros, Bahamas.

4. Pillar coral (*Dendrogyra cylindricus*); upper forereef terrace (30 to 35 feet); Discovery Bay, Jamaica.

5. Cavernous star coral (*Montastrea cavernosa*) close-up with polyps retracted; Discovery Bay, Jamaica.

6. Smooth-ridged brain coral (*Diploria strigosa*); forereef terrace (50 to 60 feet); Discovery Bay, Jamaica.

PLATE II: CARIBBEAN SCLERACTINIAN CORALS (p. 114)

1. Labyrinth or grooved brain coral (*Diploria labyrinthiformis*) close-up; Cozumel, Mexico.

2. Butter print or tan brain coral (*Meandrina meandrites*); forereef terrace (60 to 70 feet); Cozumel, Mexico.

3. Butter print or tan brain coral (*Meandrina meandrites*) close-up; Cozumel, Mexico.

4. Butter print or tan brain coral (*Meandrina meandrites*) at night; lagoon (25 to 30 feet); Discovery Bay, Jamaica.

5. Finger coral (*Porites porites*); forereef terrace (25 to 35 feet); Discovery Bay, Jamaica.

6. Mustard hill coral (*Porites astreoides*) close-up; backreef (5 to 10 feet); Belize.

7. Flower coral (*Eusmilia fastigiata*) close-up; Belize.

8. Flower coral (*Eusmilia fastigiata*) close-up with polyps extended at night; Belize.

PLATE III: CORALS AROUND THE WORLD (p. 115)

1. Plate or sheet coral (*Agaricia* sp., possibly *A. lamarcki*); forereef escarpment (60 to 90 feet); Belize.

2. Lettuce coral (*Agaricia agaricites*); forereef terrace (60 to 70 feet); Belize.

3. Pencil coral (*Madracis mirabilis*) close-up with polyps extended; lagoon, Discovery Bay, Jamaica.

4. Pacific species of staghorn and horny plate coral (*Acropora* sp.); Great Barrier Reef, Australia.

5. Orange tube coral (*Tubastraea* sp.) close-up with polyps extended; Truk Lagoon, Micronesia.

6. Bubble coral (*Plerogyra*) close-up; Maldives.

7. Leather coral (*Sarcophyton*) close-up; Great Barrier Reef, Australia.

8. Tree coral (*Dendronephthya*) close-up; Truk Lagoon, Micronesia.

PLATE IV: SOFT CORALS AND SEA ANEMONES (p. 116)

1. Crimson sea whip (*Junculla*); forereef (60 to 90 feet); Red Sea.

2. Deep water sea fan (*Iciligorgia schrammi*) close-up showing polyps with eight tentacles; Cozumel, Mexico.

3. Sea feather gorgonian coral (*Pseudopterogorgonia* sp.); shallow forereef (25 to 35 feet); Andros, Bahamas.

4. Bottle brush black coral (*Antipathes pennacea*); forereef escarpment (90 feet), Belize.

5. Giant caribbean anemone (*Condylactis gigantea*); backreef lagoon (20 to 25 feet); Discovery Bay, Jamaica.

6. Green colonial anemone (*Zoanthus sociatus*) close-up; shallow backreef lagoon (3 to 5 feet); Discovery Bay, Jamaica.

PLATE V: SEA ANEMONES AND HYDROZOANS (p. 117)

1. Orange colonial anemone (*Parazoanthus swiftii*) in green finger sponge (*Iotrochota birotulata*) close-up; backreef (10 to 15 feet); Discovery Bay, Jamaica.

2. Encrusting colonial anemone (*Palythoa caribaeorum*); shallow forereef terrace (20-30 feet); Discovery Bay, Jamaica.

3. Green colonial anemone (*Zoanthus sociatus*) and giant Caribbean anemone (*Condylactis gigantea*); backreef lagoon (25 to 35 feet); Discovery Bay, Jamaica.

4. Bladed fire coral (*Millepora complanata*); backreef (18 to 25 feet); Discovery Bay, Jamaica.

5. Crenellated fire coral (*Millepora alcicornis*); reef crest (5 to 15 feet); Andros, Bahamas.

6. Purple lace coral (*Stylaster*) close-up; forereef, Cozumel, Mexico.

PLATE VI: SPONGES (p. 118)

1. Yellow tube sponges (*Ianthella* sp.); Cozumel.

2. Red encrusting demosponge closeup; Belize.

3. "Touch-me-not" sponge (*Neofibularia nolitangere*); buttress zone, Runaway Bay, Jamaica.

4. Brown cup sponge (*Agelus* sp.); forereef escarpment (65 to 70 feet); Discovery Bay, Jamaica.

5. Sclerosponge (*Ceratoporella nicholsoni*); forereef escarpment (90 feet); Runaway Bay, Jamaica.

6. Yellow boring sponges (*Siphonodictyon coralliphagum*) in brain coral; Cozumel.

PLATE VII: PRIMARY PRODUCERS (p. 119)

1. Sea bottles or silver ball algae (*Valonia ventricosa*); lagoon, Columbus Park, Jamaica.

2. Green bubble algae (*Dictyosphaeria cavernosa*); Belize.

3. Green plate algae (*Halimeda* sp.); Discovery Bay, Jamaica.

4. Red articulated algae (*Amphiroa* sp.); Cozumel.

5. Stomatolite built by cyanobacteria with *Sargassum* (brown algae) on upper surface of mound; Lee Stocking Island, Bahamas.

6. Turtle grass (*Thalassia testudinum*); lagoon, Discovery Bay, Jamaica.

7. Distinctive prop roots of the red mangrove (*Rhizophora mangle*) along tidal inlets; Great Exuma, Bahamas.

8. Vertical air roots (pneumatophores) of the black mangrove (*Avicennia nitida*) along salt pond; Norman's Pond Cay, Bahamas.

PLATE VIII: MISCELLANEOUS INVERTEBRATES (WORMS, ARTHROPODS, MOLLUSKS) (p. 120)

1. Feather-duster worms (*Sabella melanostiguma*); Cozumel.

2. Horned or feathered Christmas tree worm (*Spirobranchus giganteus*); Jamaica.

3. Red-tipped bristle (fire) worm (*Chloeia viridis*); Discovery Bay, Jamaica.

4. Spotted sea hare (*Aplysia dactylomela*); Columbus Park, Discovery Bay, Jamaica.

5. Chiton; Lee Stocking Island, Bahamas.

6. Blue lettuce slug (*Tridachia crispata*); lagoon, Discovery Bay, Jamaica.

7. Flamingo tongues (*Cyphoma gibbosum*); lagoon, Discovery Bay, Jamaica.

8. Spiny spider crab (*Mithrax spinosissimus*); forereef, Discovery Bay, Jamaica.

1

2

3

4

5

6

COLOR PLATE I

✦ 113 ✦

1

2

3

4

5

6

7

8

COLOR PLATE II

✦ 114 ✦

COLOR PLATE III

COLOR PLATE IV
✦ 116 ✦

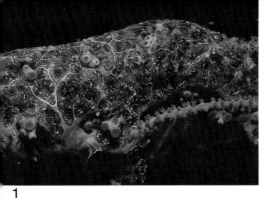

1

2

3

4

5

6

COLOR PLATE V

✦ 117 ✦

COLOR PLATE VII

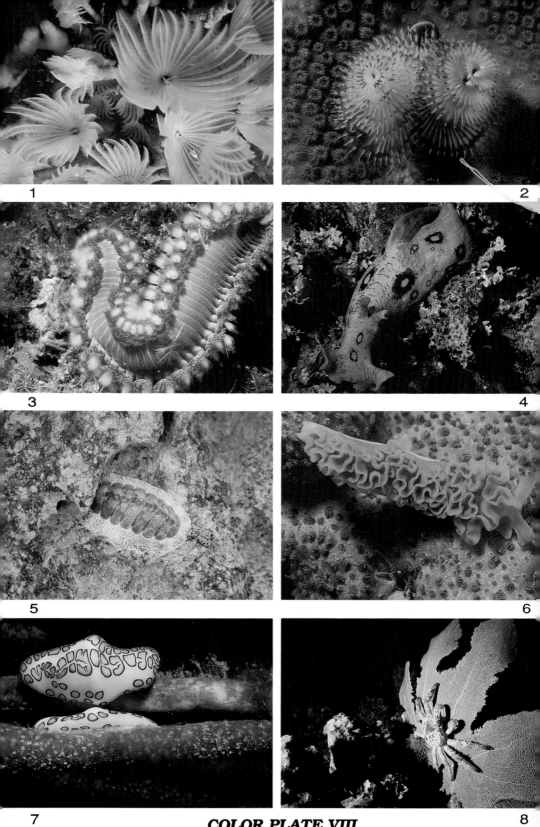

1

2

3

4

5

6

7

COLOR PLATE VIII

✦ 120 ✦

8

1

2

3

4

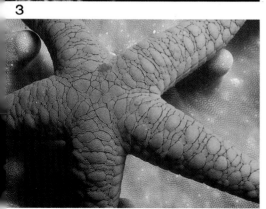

5

6

COLOR PLATE IX

✦ 121 ✦

1

2

3

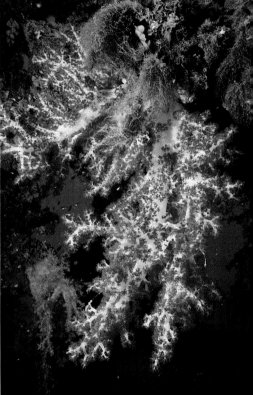

4

5

6

1

2

3

4

5

6

1

2

3

4

5

COLOR PLATE XII

✦ 124 ✦

1

2

3

COLOR PLATE XIII

4

1

2

3

4

5

6

7

8

COLOR PLATE XIV

♦ 126 ♦

COLOR PLATE XVI

✦ 128 ✦

PLATE IX: MISCELLANEOUS INVERTEBRATES (MOLLUSKS, ECHINODERMS, TUNICATES) (p. 121)

1. Long-spined, black urchin (*Diadema antillarum*); lagoon, Discovery Bay, Jamaica.
2. Basket star (*Astrophyton muricatum*); forereef terrace, Discovery Bay, Jamaica.
3. Orange sea lily (*Nemaster rubiginosa*); Belize.
4. Giant reef clam (*Tridacna gigas*); Green Island, Great Barrier Reef, Australia.
5. Orange sea star (*Fromia elegans*); Maldives.
6. Green-tipped sea squirts (ascidians); Maldives.

PLATE X: REEFS OF THE PACIFIC (p. 122)

1. Anemonefish (Skunk Clownfish, *Amphiprion perideraion*) and their host anemone (*Heteractis magnifica*); Great Barrier Reef, Australia.
2. White-tipped Reef Shark; Ribbon reefs, Great Barrier Reef, Australia.
3. Diverse branching coral growth on a shallow, steep wall; Great Barrier Reef, Australia.
4. Soft tree coral growth on a World War II wreck in Truk Lagoon.
5. Shallow reef flat, dominated by horned plate corals; Great Barrier Reef, Australia.
6. Shallow "ship reef" (*Da Nai Hino Maru*); Truk Lagoon.

PLATE XI: REEFS OF THE WORLD (p. 123)

1. Shallow reef crest with butterfly fish; Red Sea.
2. Diverse shallow coral growth; Red Sea.
3. World War II shipwreck; Truk Lagoon.
4. Deep-water red sea fan and orange finger sponges; Andros, Bahamas.
5. Schools of anchovies; Red Sea.
6. Shallow reef crest dominated by fire coral; Andros, Bahamas.

PLATE XII: CARIBBEAN REEF ZONATION (p. 124)

1. Lagoonal sand flats with ghost shrimp (*Callianassa*) mounds; 15 feet, Lee Stocking Island, Bahamas.
2. Reef crest with elkhorn coral (*Acropora palmata*); 3 feet, Andros, Bahamas.
3. Reef crest Rubble Zone between lagoon and forereef, formed by Hurricanes Allen and Gilbert; Braco, Jamaica.
4. Rear Zone of the reef crest with finger coral (*Porites porites*) and turtle grass (*Thalassia testudinum*); 3 to 5 feet, Discovery Bay, Jamaica.
5. Staghorn coral (*Acropora cervicornis*) rubble; shallow forereef, 10 to 20 feet, Lee Stocking Island, Bahamas.
6. Forereef terrace with pillar coral (*Dendrogyra cylindrus*); 25 feet, Runaway Bay, Jamaica.

PLATE XIII: CARIBBEAN REEF ZONATION (p. 125)

1. Giant stromatolite mound formed by cyanobacteria in high velocity tidal current regime; Lee Stocking Island, Bahamas.

2. Deep forereef terrace; 50 to 60 feet, east side of Discovery Bay, Jamaica.

3. Shallow forereef terrace; 35 to 40 feet, Discovery Bay, Jamaica.

4. The "Wall" or deep forereef, developed in shallower water than usual because of submerged ancient river valley; 80 feet, Rio Bueno, Jamaica.

PLATE XIV: REEF IMPACT (p. 126)

1. Fast "cat" leaving for Great Barrier Reef from Port Douglas, north of Cairns, Australia.

2. Damselfish "farm;" Columbus Park, Discovery Bay, Jamaica.

3. Black band disease; 60 foot Reef, Lee Stocking Island, Bahamas.

4. Coral destroyed by bomb; Red Sea.

5. Pipeline leading to the north coast; near Ocho Rios, Jamaica.

6. Plastic bag wrapped around elkhorn coral causing suffocation; Andros, Bahamas.

7. Photographer stirring up bottom at Cod Hole; Great Barrier Reef, Australia.

8. Submerged, coral-encrusted pipeline; leading from factory in Saipan.

PLATE XV: REEF IMPACT (p. 127)

1. Dive guide feeding grouper; Andros, Bahamas.
2. Damage caused by careless anchoring; Andros, Bahamas.
3. Dredging and filling to expand land area; Male, Maldives.
4. Fish pot on forereef terrace; Discovery Bay, Jamaica.
5. Staghorn coral stripped by carnivorous snail; Runaway Bay, Jamaica.
6. Bleached plate coral; Discovery Bay, Jamaica.

PLATE XVI: SINAI, RED SEA REEF (p. 128)

CHAPTER 9

REEF ASSOCIATES II

UNATTACHED BOTTOM DWELLERS

Among the permanent inhabitants of the coral reef community is an enormous and varied group of fixed or sessile benthic animals. The diversity of the attached reef associates exceeds that found anywhere else in nature.

The mobile or "vagrant" bottom creatures spend their lives in pursuit of prey, gliding self-propelled across the sea floor. Others stop to graze on algae covering the coral rocks. The unattached bottom dwellers include mollusks (snails, clams, scallops, octopus); arthropods (lobsters, shrimp, crabs); echinoderms (sea urchins, starfish, sea lilies, basket stars); and even a few worms.

WORMS

The sessile tube worms transcend all other worms on the coral reef in their iridescent beauty. Feathered Christmas tree worms and elegant fan worms embellish the crenellated corals with brilliant raiment. Although these sessile dandies are the most obvious worms living within the hard-coral framework, they are far from being the only worms on the reef.

Many different worm phyla may be observed moving about the reef. The ribbon worms of the Phylum Nemertea, for example, can often be found in sponges or coral rubble.

They are about as attractive as a mound of spaghetti strands, which they strongly resemble.

These so-called proboscis worms are distinguished by their flattened and elongated shape, and retractable proboscis. Another common group of marine worms contains the flat worms of the Phylum Platyhelminthes found hiding under rocks in shallow waters. When searching for prey, they move in a sluggish, side to side crawl. There are also the errant polychaetes of the Phylum Annelida, the reef's motile predators, which seem to be in constant pursuit of prey. However, of all the free-living worms inching about the reef, the most common is the polychaete fire or bristle worm.

The fire worms are the most pugnacious polychaetes on the reef. This brightly colored, segmented worm promenades boldly across the reef, attacking viciously when a target of opportunity presents itself. Its boldness to a large extent is attributed to the tufted fringe of venomous white bristles that girdles its body. These brittle setae puncture and break off at the slightest touch, injecting a venomous substance into the victim's tissue. When touched by a human, the setae can produce symptoms of burning, itching, and numbing and result in an infection. The tiny barbed bristles are difficult to remove, although it is possible to pull the setae from the skin with adhesive tape.

This vicious carnivore has a toothed tubular pharynx and it feeds by everting this device to capture prey. The worm secretes a digestive enzyme over its victim, then sucks up the partially digested meal. Fire worms are voracious coral eaters and are quite capable of digesting large quantities of living coral polyps each night. This nocturnal predator is particularly fond of the tips of the Caribbean staghorn coral, *Acropora cervicornis*, but it attacks gorgonian polyps and other soft corals as well. The segmented worms are believed to share a common ancestor with members of the Phylum Mollusca.

PHYLUM MOLLUSCA

The mollusks include a variety of remarkable creatures, which appear totally different and are separated into several classes. Each class represents a specialized adaptation to a different way of life as well as different food

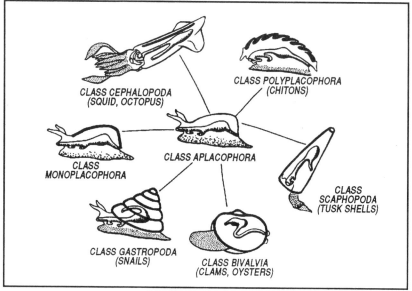

CLASS CEPHALOPODA
(SQUID, OCTOPUS)

CLASS POLYPLACOPHORA
(CHITONS)

CLASS
MONOPLACOPHORA

CLASS APLACOPHORA

CLASS
SCAPHOPODA
(TUSK SHELLS)

CLASS GASTROPODA
(SNAILS)

CLASS BIVALVIA
(CLAMS, OYSTERS)

Molluscan classes.

sources. In spite of these differences, all mollusks have complete digestive systems, nervous systems, and circulatory systems with a three-chambered heart. Variations in the shell, foot, and other soft-body parts determine the class of each mollusk.

Chitons

The chiton is a primitive mollusk of the Class Polyplacophora. This tiny polyplacophoran has a slightly arched, protective shell of eight calcareous plates held together by a fleshy girdle. Although it lives at all depths, it is commonly found on algae-covered rocks just above the high-water mark. There the chiton browses on moist algae using a snail-like mouth complete with a grinding band of magnetite teeth (**radula**). The chiton seems perfectly adapted to a life of rasping algae from rocks.

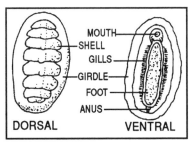

Polyplacophora (chiton).

Because it commonly lives in a zone of high-energy wave action, the chiton has a strong muscular foot with which it can clamp down te- naciously when disturbed. The very algae it feeds upon grow on the chiton's shell as well, providing an ideal camouflage.

Gastropods

Far more common and diverse are the nudibranchs, whelks, abalone, conchs, limpets, and other snails of the Class Gastropoda ("gastro" meaning stomach and "poda" meaning "foot"). A few gastropods have developed the ability to swim and some are sessile, but most crawl about the sea floor in search of food. Many gastropods are herbivores and feed only on available plants. Others are primarily carnivores eating coral polyps and any other flesh available. They have been observed boring into clam shells

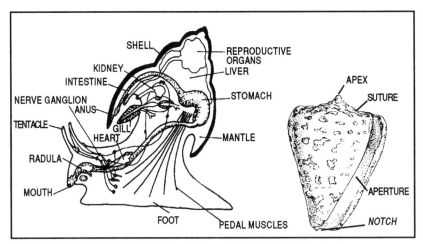

Gastropod anatomy.

(and shells of other animals) with their radula to attack the animal inside.

Unlike the bilaterally symmetrical chiton, the body and commonly the shell of the gastropod are coiled. With the body's helical twist, the animal's center of gravity is effectively lowered, enabling it to crawl on its broad muscular foot. Cone shells, cowries, and conchs are but a few of the gastropods that may be observed around the reef.

Nudibranchs and sea slugs have shed their protective shells in exchange for more efficient locomotion. To protect themselves from predators, nudibranchs rely on camouflage, coloration, and unfired nematocysts rasped from fire corals. These gastropods typically browse on the surface of the coral, whereas bivalved mollusks have adapted to burrowing.

Bivalves

Bivalves are mollusks with two shells (clams, mussels, oysters, and scallops), consequently the name Class Bivalvia. Many bi-valves live in the soft sediment as filter feeders, grazers, or burrowers, though a few attach to soft corals and hard surfaces or bore into hard rock substrates or wood. The bivalved shell, powerful adductor muscles, siphons, and loss of the molluscan head are all adaptations to burrowing or boring.

The typical burrowing bivalves have two short tubes, an incurrent siphon and an excurrent siphon, used for aspirating water through the body. These clams are

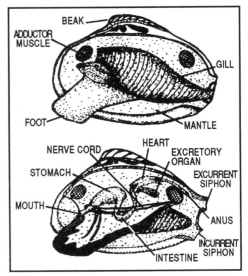

Bivalved mollusk anatomy.

deposit feeders, grazing on organic matter in the sediment. Such bivalves are commonly found with gastropods in grass beds bordering coral reefs.

Oysters, scallops, and some clams live on or near the surface and are filter feeders. Except oysters, most bivalves are mobile to some degree. Oysters have adapted to a sessile life, cemented to the substrate, where they form large colonies.

In contrast to the oysters, scallops have a remarkable swimming movement created by opening and closing their valves until they find a place to attach. They have developed tentacles and modified their musculature as well as their shape to suit their swimming life style.

On the reef itself, the patient underwater observer will find giant clams, oysters, razor clams, and pin shells associated with flamingo tongue snails, nudibranchs, other mollusks, and arthropods.

PHYLUM ARTHROPODA

Each member of the Phylum Arthropoda has jointed appendages, a hard exoskeleton, and a head, thorax, and abdomen. The appendages may include swimmerets (swim paddles) and walking legs used for locomotion and respiration, and jaws, claws, and sensory antennae that are used for food gathering.

Most marine arthropods (lobsters, crabs, shrimp, and barnacles) belong to the Class Crustacea. The crustaceans are further divided into 31

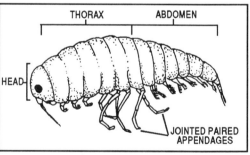

Arthropod anatomy.

orders, of which only crabs, lobsters, shrimp, and isopods are commonly found moving across the reef. All have one thing in common: for the animal to grow, periodically it must shed its hard exoskeleton.

Order Decapoda

Perhaps the largest and most common crustaceans are the decapods, which include shrimp, prawns, lobsters, and crabs. Members of this order

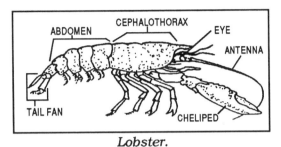

Lobster.

are distinguished by their thick shell, called a carapace, which covers their fused head and thorax (cephalothorax) bearing five pairs of walking legs.

Order Stomatopoda

Unlike the cephalothorax of the lobster and other decapods, which possess a solidly fused head and thorax, the mantis shrimp, *Squilla* has a jointed head that moves independently of its flattened body. Like the praying mantis for which it is named, it can attack swiftly with large claw-like appendages to capture and kill prey. It lives in deep burrows in the soft substrate. Mantis shrimp are common on coral reefs throughout the world. In the Caribbean alone, an estimated 60 species thrive. Isopods also have claw-like appendages.

Order Isopoda

Isopods are small crustaceans that can parasitize a wide range of reef fish, although they are most commonly seen on the heads of squirrelfish or blackbar soldierfish. Using their sharp claws to attach themselves to the host fish's head, the parasitic isopods then puncture and feed on the fish's tissue. Divers often

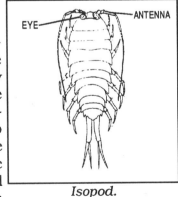

Isopod.

see the parasite, *Anilocra*, riding on the forehead of fish. It always positions itself above the eyes, facing in the same direction as its host. Other isopods, such as the sea lice, can be found scavenging around the reef, crawling over the sandy or rocky bottom.

Special Relationships

In addition to parasitic isopods, whose relationship to other creatures is obvious, several decapods have developed special relationships with other animals. The hermit crab, for example, protects its fleshy abdomen by hiding in a snail shell, which it carries around on its back until the shell is outgrown. The hermit crab enjoys an extraordinary relationship with sea anemones as well. Some hermit crabs carry anemones on their shells and even transfer the anemone when an outgrown shell is replaced. The anemone receives transportation, while the crab benefits from additional protection in this unusual example of mutualism.

The giant decorator crab also encourages encrusting organisms to grow on its carapace and transfers them when it sheds its exoskeleton. In this way it is camouflaged from predators and prey.

Several shrimp have mutually-beneficial (commensal) relationships with other animals. Pederson's cleaning shrimp removes minute ectoparasites from host fish and other marine creatures. The snapping shrimp snaps his big claw closed with a clicking sound, which biologists believe serves as a warning to other shrimp and, simultaneously, attracts prey. The snapping shrimp often makes the ringed sea anemone its lair. Commensal relationships are less common in the Phylum Echinodermata.

Banded coral shrimp.

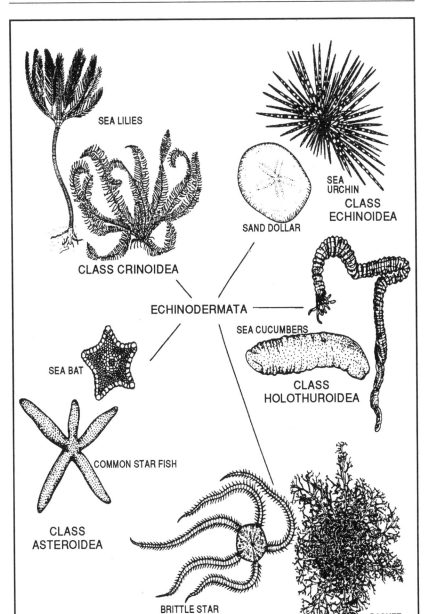

SEA LILIES

CLASS CRINOIDEA

SAND DOLLAR

SEA URCHIN

CLASS ECHINOIDEA

ECHINODERMATA

SEA CUCUMBERS

CLASS HOLOTHUROIDEA

SEA BAT

COMMON STAR FISH

CLASS ASTEROIDEA

BRITTLE STAR

CLASS OPHIUROIDEA

BASKET STAR

Diversity in the Phylum Echinodermata.

PHYLUM ECHINODERMATA

Members of the Phylum Echinodermata seem at first glance to be totally unrelated, yet the hundreds of different species of echinoderms, of which sea urchins, starfish, brittle stars, basket stars, sea cucumbers, feather stars, sand dollars, and sea lilies are but a few, have much in common. The echinoderms ("echino" meaning spiny, "derm" meaning skin) are benthic organisms with internal skeletons comprised of calcareous plates and a water vascular system. This unique system enables most echinoderms to move about efficiently on tiny tube feet powered by hydraulic pressure.

Five-sided radial symmetry is considered a characteristic of the phylum, though the larvae and some of the more mobile adults (sea cucumbers and heart urchins) have noticeable *bilateral symmetry*. A fascinating characteristic shared by sea cucumbers, sea lilies, brittle stars and starfish is the ability to regenerate body parts that have been lost.

Members of this phylum are varied in their feeding habits. Many are herbivores and are commonly found grazing on reef algae. Others are voracious predators and if unchecked can quickly decimate a reef.

Class Asteroidea

Among the most aggressive carnivores on the reef are the starfish or sea stars of the Class Asteroidea. The asteroids have five or more arms used for food gathering. The underside of each arm is covered with rows of hundreds of tiny tube feet with suction disks at the ends.

Many sea stars favor the bivalved mollusk as a food source. These starfish use their sucker feet to pull the shells of bivalves apart, while inserting their diaphanous stomachs through a thin gap between the shells. The stomachs secrete digestive enzymes that effectively break down molluscan tissue, which the sea stars then aspirate.

Several years ago, oyster fishermen, understandably angered by the sea stars' heavy predation on their oyster beds, tried to kill the sea stars by cutting them in half and disposing of them in the sea. Regrettably for the fishermen, far from having the desired effect, the sea stars regrew the missing parts and multiplied accordingly. Sea stars have also been observed dining on a broad menu of crabs, worms, barnacles, sponges and even brittle stars.

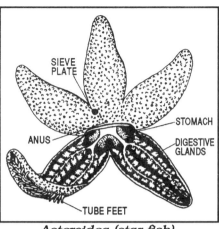

Asteroidea (star fish).

Labels: SIEVE PLATE, STOMACH, ANUS, DIGESTIVE GLANDS, TUBE FEET

Acanthaster, the crown-of-thorns starfish, has been regarded as the most devastating predator on Pacific coral reefs. So ravenous is its appetite for the flesh of coral polyps that, during a 2-year period when it was unchecked, it destroyed nearly 90 percent of the corals surrounding the island of Guam.

Sea stars are found in eelgrass or turtlegrass beds, in shallow sandy areas, or tucked inside the cracks and crevices of coral reefs. Although large, mature sea stars have few natural enemies; the young are vulnerable to predation by the giant triton snail, sponge crabs, shrimp, and larger fish such as the grouper.

Class Ophiuroidea

The members of Class Ophiuroidea, including brittle stars and basket stars, bear some resemblance to the sea stars, but have a distinct central disk and much thinner arms. Compared to the thick, stiff arms of the sea star, the brittle star's arms are long and delicate. Radiating from the central area are five long, snake-like arms used for locomotion. The arms are lined with short tube feet that function as sensory organs and aid in respiration.

Brittle Stars

Brittle stars, the most mobile of echinoderms, can scuttle with agility or swim briefly as the spirit moves them. With rapid, whip-like movements of its arms, the brittle star can even ensnare tiny worms and crustaceans. Because the writhing of their arms has been likened to the serpentine movement of a snake, they have also been called serpent stars.

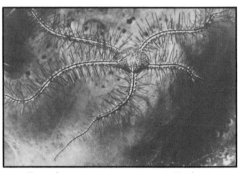

Brittle star on sponge, Belize.

The name "brittle star" describes its fragile nature because their arms are easily broken off when handled. This may be a natural escape mechanism to confuse attackers while the brittle star makes a getaway.

On the underside of its body is a mouth containing five triangular jaws with tooth-like edges. Although many brittle stars capture tiny animals by filter feeding, others forage through the soft sediment for organic detritus.

Brittle stars are well represented on most coral reefs, but being small, shy, and nocturnal, they appear less numerous than they really are. They fancy the dark crevices offered by the corals and sponges. However, under the cover of darkness, the brittle stars climb to the top of their hideaway to feed. It is not unusual to count several dozen brittle stars on a single vase sponge at night!

Basket Stars

Significantly different from the brittle star in appearance, the basket star is observed in all its splendor only at night. Hidden away in some dark coral crevasse or silently entangled in gorgonians by day, in the dark of night it climbs slowly to the top of the reef battlements. Here it attaches firmly to the crest of a sea feather or sea fan and slowly deploys an extraordinary parachute of slender tendrils. This complex network secretes threads of sticky mucus that strain microscopic plankton from the water.

The basket star shuns the diver's light. Shine your beam on it too long, and its elegant tendrils recoil into an imperceptible ball of organic spaghetti.

Class Crinoidea

The crinoids or sea lilies, like the basket stars, are among the most efficient filter feeders on the reef. Of the five major classes within the echinoderm phylum, crinoids are the only class with some sessile forms. The others all contain animals that are unattached and move around the reef.

Attached crinoids were far more abundant in the past, and in fact, the geologic record contains evidence that vast meadows of stalked sea lilies once covered much of the sea floor. The stalked crinoids exist today only at great depths and are the descendants of the remarkable stalked sessile echinoderms that survived extinction 200 million years ago.

Living in shallow water, the stalkless crinoids (also known as feather stars) are mobile and can swim modestly with up-and-down movements of their arms. These crinoids have relatively small bodies and use finger-like cirri to crawl short distances or to perch on sponges or high peaks on the reef.

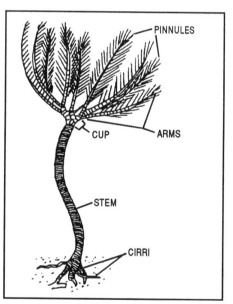

Crinoid.

A few stalkless, motile crinoids have adapted quite successfully to life on the shallow coral reef. Shunning sunlight, many crinoids hide from predators by day, but at night they climb high on the reef and spread their arms wide to strain plankton and organic detritus from the water. Grooves, lined by finger-like pinnules covered with tube feet, whisk the food to a central mouth.

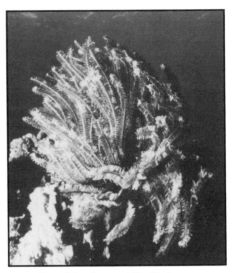

Sea lily (crinoid), Saipan.

Crinoids are not exclusively nocturnal throughout the world. In the Caribbean, for example, crinoids expose their arms, but not their bodies, during the day; and in the waters around Australia and Micronesia, some crinoids are commonly exposed during the day. However, in the Red Sea crinoids emerge only after dark and are never seen by day.

The remarkable crinoids are among the most advanced reef dwellers living on the bottom. In contrast to the small body and elaborate arms of the crinoid, sea urchins have large, inflated bodies covered with spines.

Class Echinoidea

The echinoids (sea urchins, sea biscuits, heart urchins, and sand dollars) are unique among the echinoderms. They illustrate how adaptation to environment and lifestyle can modify appearance. Echinoids have no arm-like appendages and have modified their bodies to a ball shape that may be elongated. All echinoids have spines that may discourage predators. Depending on species, they may have long sharp spines, or short stout spines.

The sea urchin's internal skeleton is made up of fused calcareous plates arranged in nearly perfect radial symmetry.

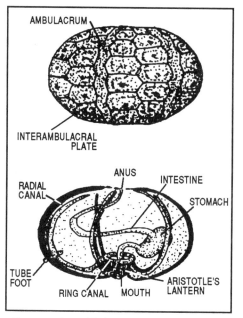

Sea urchin (Echinoidea) anatomy.

Along the upper side are a functional anus and five rows of tube feet commonly used for respiration.

Like the sea star, echinoids also have five rows of tube feet on their underside. Because the tube feet extend beyond the spines, they can be used with the spines to crawl. Many echinoids also have a jaw-like chewing mouth called Aristotle's lantern located on the ventral side.

Sea urchins are hardy eaters and can scrape algae from the reef rocks at a rate that belies their slow-moving nature. During this process, they significantly erode hard reef surfaces. Because they are herbivores, sea urchins are commonly found grazing the grass beds as well as the reef.

Short-spined white urchin, Jamaica.

Diadema antillarum

One of the most common reef-dwelling urchins in the Caribbean has been *Diadema antillarum*. The long spines of this common black urchin are needle sharp and brittle. Many a careless diver has learned just how sharp and brittle by brushing against one and finding its spines broken off under his skin. When the spines break, they release a mild, purple-colored venom, which is probably in the same toxicity range as that of the honeybee. Any discomfort caused by the venom is easily tolerated by most humans and dissipates quickly. The particles of spine quickly dissolve and are absorbed by the body within a few days.

The importance of *Diadema* to the reef's continued health must not be underestimated. The spiny sea urchin is a significant herbivore in the complex reef ecosystem. To a large extent, *Diadema* may well be a key control on growth of algae, a fact becoming increasingly evident in the Caribbean and Florida Keys following the 1983 mass dieoff described earlier. From the carnivorous predators, such as the queen triggerfish and jolthead porgys that feed on *Diadema*, to the wide range of algae the urchins help control, the impact of *Diadema* on the ecological balance of the reef is only just beginning to be understood.

In addition to symmetrical surface-dwelling sea urchins, there is another group of sea urchins to be considered.

Burrowers

Many of those urchins living within the substrate have modified their shapes substantially to accommodate a lifestyle as a burrower. The so-called "irregular" urchin has replaced radial symmetry with bilateral symmetry. Commonly, the anus has shifted posteriorly. These sea urchins have no long, protective spines and as a result are heavily predated by crabs, helmet conchs, and fish. Consequently, they burrow into the sand to hide from predators as well as to scavenge for organic detritus.

Three major types of burrowing urchins are found in the back reef. The heart urchin lives just below the muddy sediment in shallow water, whereas in shallow backreef lagoons, small mounds of sand hide the sea pussy. The short-spined sea biscuit, which looks like a thick brush, is found grazing detritus on the sand flats or in the grass beds.

Class Holothuroidea

Members of the Class Holothuroidea are commonly known as sea cucumbers, and rarely has an animal been so descriptively named. The tubular holothurian has the echinoderm characteristic of five-sided symmetry with its five internalized longitudinal muscles. Radial symmetry has been replaced externally with bilateral symmetry to accommodate a life of foraging on sand and mud. When the sea cucumber crawls slowly across the bottom, its elongate axis parallels the sea floor.

Around the mouth at its anterior end is an encircling wreath of tentacles and sense organs. At the posterior end is a functional anus that forms the endless necklaces of fecal pellets in evidence wherever the persistent sea cucumber is in residence.

Brown-spotted sea cucumber, Jamaica

Sea cucumbers have the amazing ability to regenerate their viscera. If attacked, they can throw out (eviscerate) their internal organs to decoy and elude the attacker.

In evolving from the traditional solid, spiny internal skeleton, the sea cucumber has instead calcareous spicules embedded in its leathery hide. Sea cucumbers may appear thick and rigid, or delicate and flaccid. One species resembles a limp vacuum cleaner hose.

Regardless of their shapes, one thing is absolutely certain: many sea cucumbers are effective detritus feeders, constantly funnelling sand and mud into their mouths to extract organic material, their principal sources of food. In this way, sea cucumbers clean the reef of any dead organic matter and any bacteria that live on the organic matter. Scientists estimate that detritus-feeding sea cucumbers on a typical coral reef will cycle *all the surface sediment surrounding that reef* through their digestive tracts at least twice each year!

REEF TENANTS

The numbers and dimensions of the reef dwellers are enough to fascinate and occupy the minds of an army of scientists for a millennium. There are sufficient painted shrimps, sea slugs, and feather worms to empty the magical palettes of a thousand sorcerers' apprentices.

Still, these are only tenants, no matter how fascinating or how other-worldly, they may be. The landlord is the tiny, primitive animal that has sculpted magnificent castles in the sea. It is the coral polyp that has built this refuge in the emerald-green sea.

Sea star, Saipan

CHAPTER 10

CORAL REEFS OF THE WORLD AND THEIR ZONATIONS

Coral reefs throughout the world, regardless of form or dimension, host remarkably similar plants and animals. Although each reef is comprised of many elements, these plants and animals live in equally similar environments. Out of the darkness of the deep blue sea, great snowy white breakers come hissing to explode against formidable coral ramparts, which themselves rise abruptly from the depths of the sea.

It is a paradox that the primitive, little coral organism should be the architect of a fortification great enough to withstand the most powerful forces of the ocean. From these dizzy precipices, bands of convoluted corals sprawl, bordered by broad algal ridges. Dividing the labyrinth of reefs are the surge channels, which act as ducts through which the storm and trade-wind-blown waves flood and ebb. On the tide-emptied flats lies a great vista of coral rubble, the casualties in the never-ending assault of natural violence, and yet, in the little tidal pools abounds an amazing variety of life. To the leeward of the rubble, the clear emerald waters of the lagoon are filled with mound upon mound of corals and sprawling grass and sand flats.

The corals take many different forms, influenced in their development by regional variations as much as genetic factors. Astride massive submarine parapets are soft, lacy fronds of gorgonians sweeping in rhythm with the surge. The bases of the mighty coral buttresses are covered by great platters and basins of deep-water corals that draw only the weakest photons of light. Corals that look like plants and flowers, corals that form grottoes and gardens, corals that look like human brains, mushrooms, or the antlers of forest animals diversify the reef ecosystem, yet, the coral reefs of the world, which in their natural magnificence dwarf any of mankind's considerable achievements, are reinforced, not divided, by this diversity.

ATLANTIC AND INDO-PACIFIC REEFS

Science has spent decades delineating the differences between the coral reefs of the western Atlantic and Caribbean and those of the Indo-Pacific and Red Sea, and yet, these coral reefs - in structure, available habitat, or even relationships between reef organisms - hardly differ at all.

The reefs of each region are unique in several ways. The diversity of marine life, for example, is much greater in the Indo-Pacific. On the other hand, the exceptional transparency of the Atlantic waters has enabled coral reefs to develop at depths as great as 300 feet in many places, nearly twice as deep as most Pacific corals are found, yet there is undeniably a significantly greater diversity of hard scleractinian corals and soft alcyonarian corals in the Indo-Pacific. Not only are there more genera of corals, but also more species per genus. More than 200 species of *Acropora* alone thrive in the Indo-Pacific compared to 3 in the Atlantic!

Reef scientists theorize that the low diversity of corals may result from the Atlantic reefs being mere thin veneers over earlier reefs that barely survived the last glacial age more than 10,000 years ago. The greater impact of glaciation on the Atlantic Ocean is attributed to its smaller size. Interestingly, water temperatures during the last glacial advance were no more than 5° F colder than the water temperatures of today. That means coral reef growth would not have ended. With the post-glacial rise in sea level, however, many coral reefs apparently drowned and nutrients and turbidity associated with runoff from flooded lands slowed coral growth. Still, many reefs were able to match growth rates with increasing water levels and thrive. There is evidence to indicate Atlantic corals are generally less wave resistant and smaller than the corals of the Indo-Pacific, although the Atlantic and Pacific Oceans have only become separated during the past 7 million years. The vastly greater area of the Indo-Pacific has provided a far more stable environment and a broader range of substrate over the years, resulting in the greater diversity.

GEOGRAPHIC DISTRIBUTION OF MAJOR REEF SYSTEMS

It has been suggested that if all of the living scleractinian corals distributed throughout the world's oceans were laid side by side, they would cover an area greater than that of the combined continents of Asia, Africa, and Europe. Since one of the principal controlling factors in the growth of coral reefs is temperature, it is no surprise the geographic distribution of these reef-building corals is related to the path of the warm-ocean currents. Coral larvae are capable of drifting with a favorable ocean current for thousands of nautical miles, so the potential for colonization is remarkably high where warm ocean currents flow past the shores of tropical and subtropical land masses.

The Great Barrier Reef

Of all the mighty reefs, none is more majestic than the one that sits astride the continental shelf off Australia's northeast coast. The Great Barrier Reef is the most magnificent natural edifice ever created by living creatures. More than 1,300 miles long with variable width and depth, its waters engulf an aquatic kingdom of more than 79,585 square miles. It is far more than a single reef; it is a colossal complex of patch reefs, barrier reefs, atolls, shoals, sand dunes, islets, and islands. This world wonder is by far the largest reef complex on Earth today. To study a satellite photograph of the Great Barrier Reef is to gain a lesson in striking diversity, so great is the variation in reef development from south to north.

In the extreme south, the continental shelf is narrow and the reef is fragmented into the atoll groups of Capricorn and Bunker, divided by a maze of navigable channels. These waters are the coolest along the Great Barrier Reef and consequently coral development is more scattered. Continuing northward, the continental shelf broadens with a corresponding increase in tidal ranges. Coral growth is manifested in large platform reefs widely spaced on the seaward edge of poorly developed reef flats.

The middle reefs are comprised of large platform reefs formed along the inside of the broad continental shelf. Here also are vast reef flats and inshore mangrove islands. Farther offshore, development is limited to scattered small reefs and short ribbon reefs among the east-west-oriented patch reefs. These are the so-called deltaic reefs, because they are separated by a labyrinth of shallow, meandering channels.

Moving into the warm waters of the north, the narrow ribbon reefs form a nearly unbroken wall of coral. As the reefs lengthen (to 15 miles long and only 1,500 feet wide), the channels dividing them grow fewer and narrower. The narrow ribbon reefs lie oriented to the north and south. Reefs developing along the edge of the faulted continental shelf to the north of Cairns, are more than 15 million years old. In contrast, the other reefs in the Great Barrier Reef system are less than 2 million years old.

Central Pacific

Compared to the Atlantic and Indian Oceans, the central Pacific is characterized by a lack of continental land masses. Many Pacific islands have been formed by ancient reef growth or accumulation of reef debris surrounding volcanic centers. The Hawaiian Islands, Fiji, and French Polynesia have well developed fringing reefs, barrier reefs, and atolls. Strong storms, waves, and currents generated in the central Pacific result in shallow reefs being dominated by coralline algae.

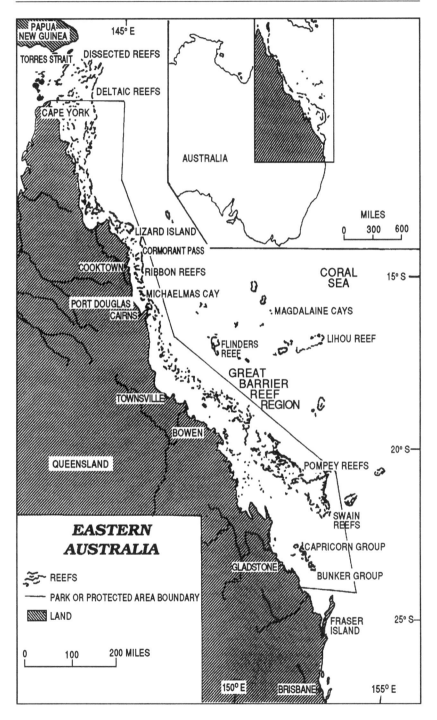

Southeast Asia

An estimated 30 percent of the world's coral reefs is found in the waters of southeast Asia and the adjoining islands. This region encompasses the countless islands of the Philippines, Borneo, and the Malay Archipelago. Most of the reefs associated with shallow coastal areas and small to medium islands are fringing reefs, but barrier reefs and atolls are represented also. The more remote the reef, the more luxuriant is the coral growth. The high sedimentation and nutrient runoff common to the waters of large coastal cities restricts healthy coral development.

Indian Ocean

There is no land bridge or other real physical barrier to separate the Pacific Ocean from the Indian Ocean, and consequently the reefs are remarkably similar. Among the more interesting reef systems in the Indian Ocean are 19 major atolls, which comprise the Maldives. These islands are at, or very near, sea level and are constantly being reshaped by nature . . . and by humans. Consequently, the waters are filled with large amounts of suspended sediment with the attendant low visibility. The best coral development is near narrow tidal inlets, where currents are strongest. The corals that best withstand the effect of the heavy currents are primarily the low, massive, or encrusting forms.

Red Sea

The Red Sea is no less than an arm of the Indian Ocean and at its northernmost end diverges into two long narrow passages, the Gulf of Suez and the Gulf of Aqaba. The land separating the two gulfs is the famous Sinai Peninsula, a land bridge that connects Asia to Africa. The Sinai continues to split away from the African continent and drift eastward. Since the Red Sea is a marginal sea of the Indian Ocean, there is a marked similarity in reef faunas.

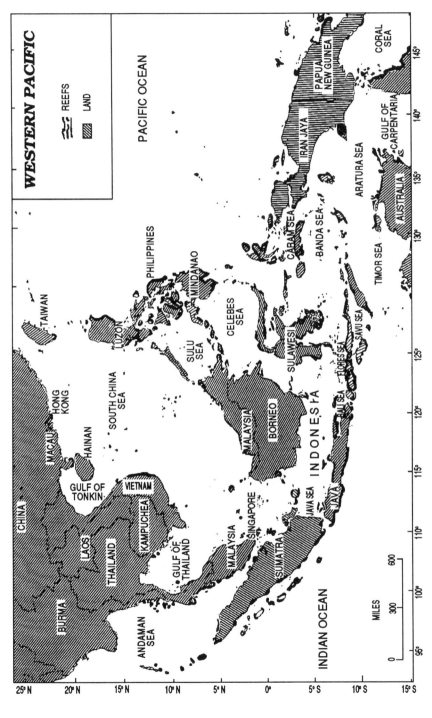

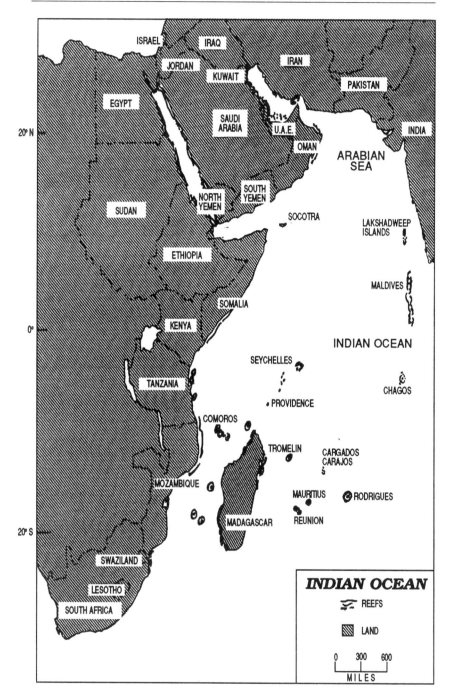

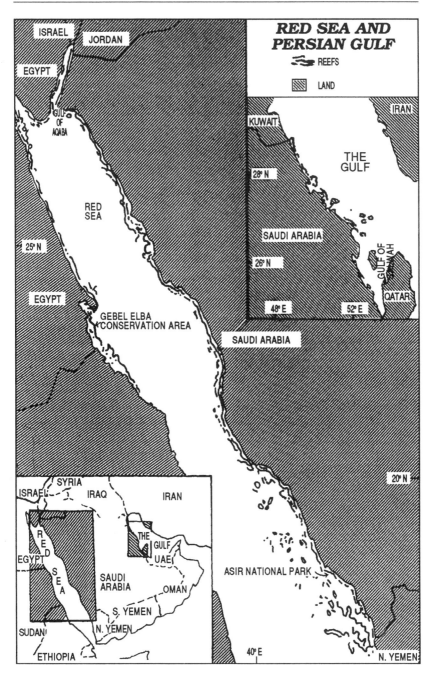

Although its salinity is greater than that of most healthy coral reef ecosystems, the Red Sea supports a diverse biota. The Gulf of Aqaba is particularly fertile, supporting a surprising array of marine flora and fauna. Reef investigators claim that more than 1,000 species of fish thrive in these luxuriant waters. So much life is packed into each cubic foot of these beautiful reefs, it is difficult to imagine a more prolific or diverse reef system anywhere in the world. Of the two gulfs, Aqaba is, by far, narrower and deeper. Along its eastern shore great fringing reefs have developed that fall away abruptly to abyssal depths as great as 3,300 feet.

Persian Gulf

Reefs of the Persian Gulf provide a marked contrast with those of the Red Sea. The coast of the Red Sea is characterized by steep dropoffs to great depths and has extensive fringing reefs. The Gulf coast, on the other hand, has vast shallow-water, muddy grass beds along the shore. Shallow depths, soft substrates, turbid waters, and extremes in temperature and salinity have resulted in limited reef growth.

Isolated reefs do occur around offshore islands in the northern Gulf, but these reefs are developed in less than 45 feet of water and have low diversities. The maximum number of coral species present is about 1/3 the number in the Red Sea and slightly less than the number in the Caribbean.

Caribbean Sea

Study a world map. With your finger trace a path from the southern United States southwestward to the east coast of Central America. Continue southeasterly along the north coast of the South American continent and then swing north and then westerly, following the long curve of islands that comprise the Greater and Lesser Antilles. When you're back at your starting point, you've roughly delineated the boundaries of the Caribbean Sea.

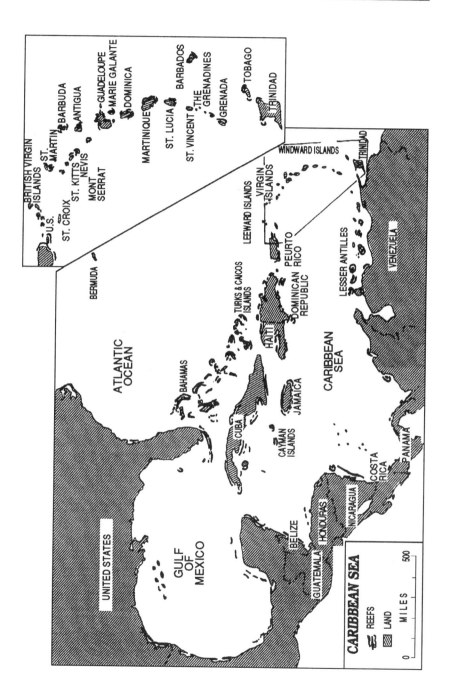

Spectacular coral reefs have formed in the shallow tropical and subtropical waters along the margins of the continents and islands in the Caribbean Sea. Throughout the Caribbean, the reef zonation reflects the respective influences of glacial sea-level changes and island tilting on the seafloor topography. Where shorelines are protected from violent wave action, extensive fringing reefs are well developed. Perhaps the most detailed study of Caribbean reef zonation has been made in Jamaica where the reefs are typically fringing reefs, although barrier and bank reefs are in evidence.

Because such islands as Jamaica and the Cayman Islands have narrow shelves with abrupt dropoffs to deep water, the fringing and barrier reefs often develop a series of caves, terraces and dramatic walls.

Areas bordering the Caribbean have exciting coral reef development as well. Among these are the reefs of the Bahamas Archipelago, the Turks and Caicos, Florida, Bermuda, and the Gulf of Mexico.

Bahamas

Although the water temperatures are generally less than optimal, the 3,000 islands that comprise the Bahamas and the Turks and Caicos support innumerable coral reefs. Engendered in this prolific reef development is a rich diversity of marine plants and animals. The Bahamas circumscribe an oceanic area 700 miles long and nearly 400 miles wide, including 5,190 square miles of marginal bank reefs and a barrier reef.

Perhaps the most impressive of all the reefs in the archipelago is the barrier reef off the Atlantic side of Andros Island, contiguous to the famed fish bowl of the western Atlantic, the Tongue of the Ocean. It is the third longest barrier reef in the world behind Australia's Great Barrier Reef and the Belize Barrier Reef and is the longest in the Atlantic Ocean.

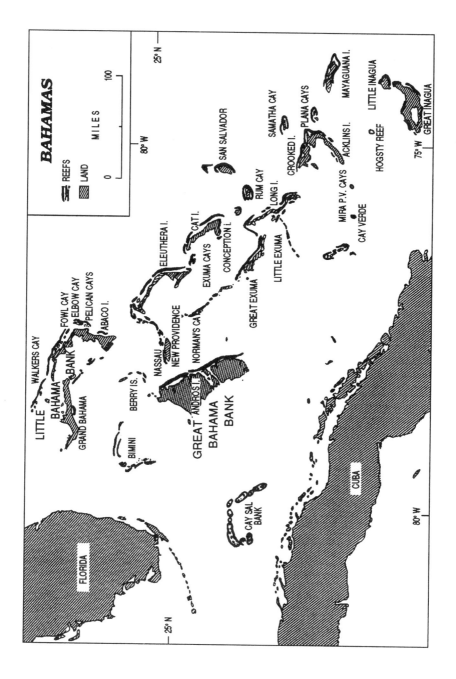

Bermuda

The coral reefs of Bermuda represent the northernmost limit of coral development in the world: that they exist at all, as impoverished as they are, is only because they are in the path of the Gulf Stream's warm waters. Even so, the typical temperature of the waters off Bermuda (68° F) is, at best, not conducive to the building of coral reefs. Because a minimum temperature of 74° F is required for branching corals to proliferate, corals such as *Acropora* that dominate southern Atlantic and Caribbean reefs are conspicuously absent from Bermuda's colder waters. A reef scientist could easily identify more than 60 coral species in the southern Caribbean around an island such as Bonaire, for example, but in Bermuda, one would be hard pressed to locate 20 species. Nevertheless, the reefs that are present are well developed and support a healthy marine flora and fauna.

Gulf of Mexico

Along the southern margin of the United States, because of the cool water temperatures and heavy influx of sediments, coral reefs are poorly developed. However, the Flower Gardens reefs, located on top of two salt domes on the Texas shelf, are the northernmost living coral reefs in the Gulf of Mexico. In the southern Gulf of Mexico, coral reef systems are well developed, and Campeche Bank and Alacran Reef off the Yucatan Peninsula provide good examples of bank and atoll reefs.

Florida

Along the eastern shoreline of Florida, beginning north of Palm Beach, a string of coral reefs makes a gentle curve southwesterly to the Dry Tortugas. The farther south the curve extends, the warmer the water and the greater the number of hard, scleractinian corals.

The reefs of the Florida Keys diverge into outer- and inner-reef tracts. The outer reefs are better developed

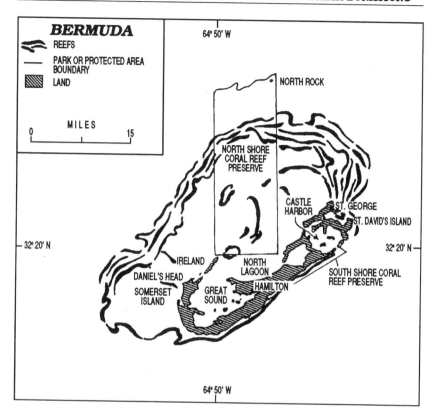

because they are adjacent to the Gulf Stream's low-nutrient waters. Like the ribbon reefs of the Great Barrier Reef, these outer reefs grow along the seaward edge of the continental shelf and host a rich and diverse marine fauna.

The inner-reef tract is comprised of small patch reefs formed in the shallows between the outer reef and the islands (keys). The islands shelter these reefs from the turbidity, low salinity, and variable temperatures of the outflow from Florida Bay. Consequently, the healthiest and best developed reefs are those that lie parallel to and offshore from the large keys, whereas only a few less healthy reefs lie south of passes between the keys.

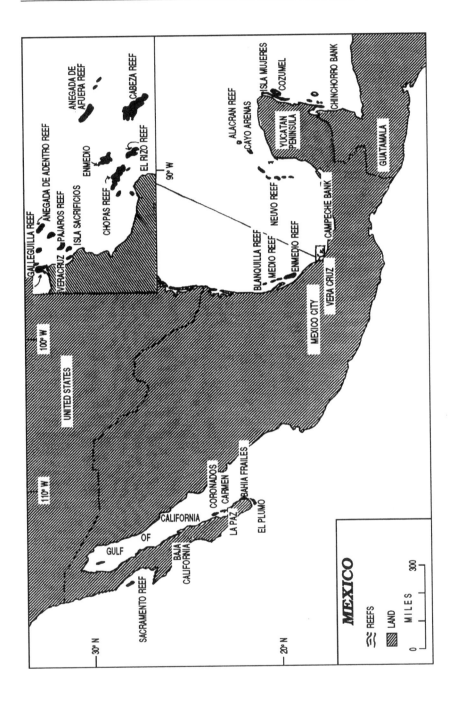

Map labels: CABEZA REEF, ANEGADA DE AFUERA REEF, ANEGADA DE ADENTRO REEF, PAJAROS REEF, ISLA SACRIFICIOS, ENMEDIO, EL RIZO REEF, CHOPAS REEF, GALLEGUILLA REEF, VERACRUZ, ISLA MUJERES, COZUMEL, CHINCHORRO BANK, ALACRAN REEF, CAYO ARENAS, YUCATAN PENINSULA, GUATAMALA, NUEVO REEF, CAMPECHE BANK, ENMEDIO REEF, BLANQUILLA REEF, MEDIO REEF, VERA CRUZ, MEXICO CITY, 90° W, 100° W, 110° W, UNITED STATES, CALIFORNIA, CORONADOS, CARMEN, BAHIA FRAILES, LA PAZ, EL PLUMO, GULF, OF, BAJA CALIFORNIA, SACRAMENTO REEF, 30° N, 20° N, MEXICO, REEFS, LAND, MILES, 0, 300

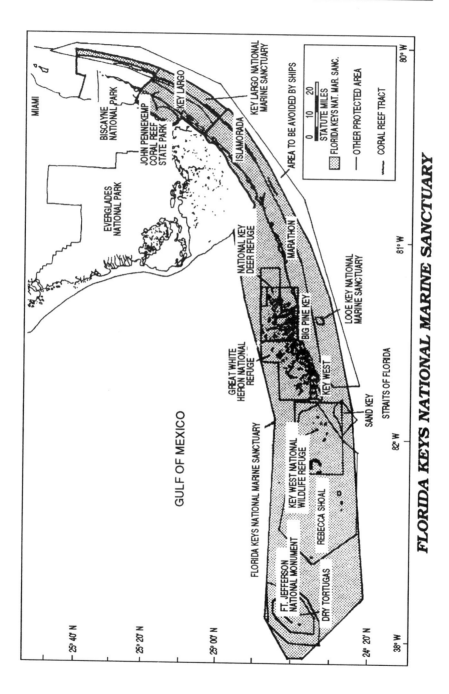

FLORIDA KEYS NATIONAL MARINE SANCTUARY

CORAL REEF ZONATION

Although clearly substantial differences exist between coral reefs in all oceans, there seems to be one undeniable common element: coral reefs throughout the world are characterized by regions of growth quite distinct from adjoining areas. Because the coral reef ecosystem is so expansive and so complicated, reef scientists have used these natural regions or **zones** to divide the reef into manageable units.

Zones

In 1959, Thomas F. Goreau, one of the pioneers of reef research, working in Jamaica, described three major regions of coral growth and then divided these regions into sub-units called zones. These zones were based on the composition of resident species and reef topography. Goreau's model has become a foundation for reef-zonation studies throughout the world. Goreau's zones are characterized not only by different marine flora and fauna, but also by the environmental differences they reflect, particularly those of light and water movement.

The shallowest region of the reef is called the **reef crest**. Although it has the greatest abundance of sunlight, coral development is limited here by the high-water energy as well as by extremes in exposure, salinity, and temperature. Typically, the reef crest has a low diversity of corals and is dominated by only one or two coral or hydrozoan species.

The **back reef** (including shore and lagoon zones of the reef system) is often a zone of considerable diversity. It is surprisingly quiet, despite its proximity to the pounding surf. It is sheltered seaward by the reef crest and leeward by the land margin.

The region seaward of the reef crest is commonly termed the **forereef**. The forereef is typically divided into several unique coral zones characterized by depth and bottom topography, which control light penetration and water movement.

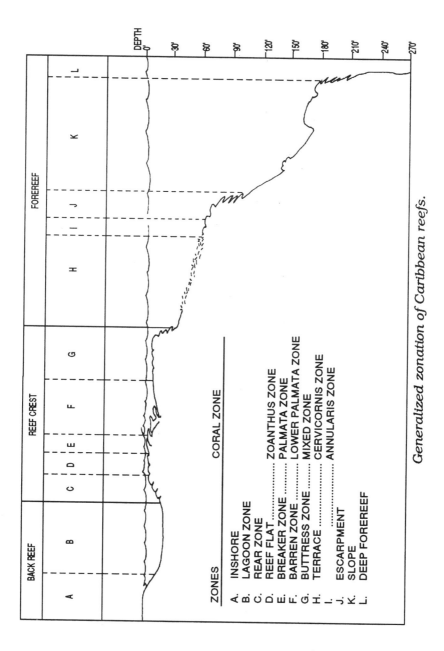

Generalized zonation of Caribbean reefs.

ZONES   CORAL ZONE

A.   INSHORE
B.   LAGOON ZONE
C.   REAR ZONE
D.   REEF FLAT .... ZOANTHUS ZONE
E.   BREAKER ZONE .... PALMATA ZONE
F.   BARREN ZONE .... LOWER PALMATA ZONE
G.   BUTTRESS ZONE .... MIXED ZONE
H.   TERRACE .... CERVICORNIS ZONE
I.   .... ANNULARIS ZONE
J.   ESCARPMENT
K.   SLOPE
L.   DEEP FOREREEF

Similar, But Different

It is a simple matter to describe the zonation of a given reef. To extend the same zonation to other reefs in other parts of the world is more difficult. Beyond the obvious ecological prerequisites of adequate sunlight and optimal water temperatures, healthy coral development demands reasonably sediment-free water, and sufficient water energy to provide an adequate oxygen supply.

Even under the best of conditions, zonation may be incomplete or poorly developed. Some deep reefs often lack the reef-crest zones, whereas other shallow reefs may have less than complete forereef zonation. Regional differences, including frequency of tropical storms, amount of coastal disturbance, tidal range, water depth, and bottom topography, also can profoundly impact reef zonation.

Caribbean Reef Zonation

Reef Crest

The reef crest is subjected to a variety of stressful environmental factors. Intense wave action and strong currents require stout coral development to withstand the high energy. Here, fast-growing branching corals with their branches oriented into the wave energy have dominion. The reef crest is not one, but a series of zones whose growth is controlled by depth and water energy.

Breaker Zone

At the seaward edge of the reef crest lies the breaker zone, the shallowest part of the reef where the full force of the ocean surf is absorbed and waves are broken. In the Caribbean, this area is also known as the palmata zone because it tends to be dominated by the massive elkhorn coral, *Acropora palmata*. On some reefs there are also dense thickets of the hydrozoan *Millepora complanata*, the

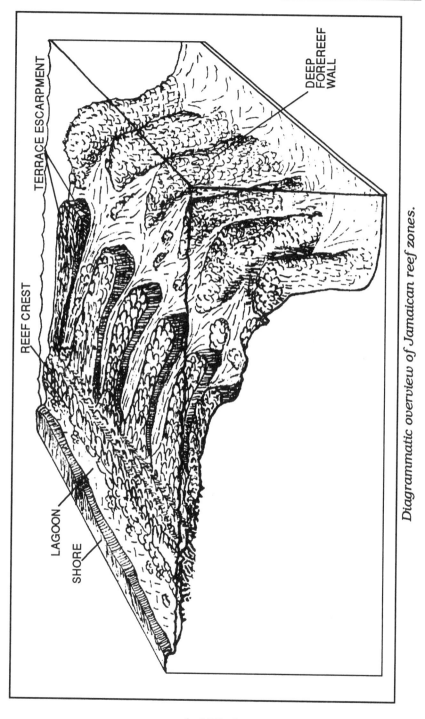

Diagrammatic overview of Jamaican reef zones.

flat-bladed fire coral. Depth in this zone typically ranges from the surface to approximately 15 feet.

Under the endless pounding of waves, surge channels have been cut into the seaward edge of the reef to accommodate the sediment-laden return flow of waves and tidal currents. The surge channels and finger-like reefs form the area that has been called the "spur-and-groove zone." On the sides of these channels only the star coral (*Montastrea*), brain coral (*Diploria*), lettuce coral (*Agaricia agaricites*), and mustard hill coral (*Porites astreoides*) are able to grow. On Bermuda and most Pacific reefs, the reef crest may be encrusted by coralline red algae. Leeward of the breaker zone is the rubble zone.

Rubble Zone

Landward from the surf zone is a high narrow rampart of reef debris called the rubble zone. Here millions of coral fragments, broken by the ocean's waves and encrusted by coralline algae, form a protective bulwark to lessen wave and storm impact on the reef flat and rear zone of the reef crest.

Reef Flat

As its name suggests, the reef flat is a zone of little vertical relief. It covers the largest expanse of the upper reef and is typically barren of coral growth. This flat, broad zone is characterized by maximum sunlight, considerable wave-energy turbulence at high tide, and, since it is near mean low tide, periods of exposure or extreme calm at low tide. At most, the reef flat is covered by a water depth of less than 3 feet.

Although a few hardy elkhorn corals may be present, harsh conditions inhibit coral development. Life on the reef flat is dominated by the sea fans, sea whips, fire corals, filamentous algal turf, and an abundance of the calcareous green alga, *Halimeda*. The reef flat is also known as the Zoanthus zone because in some areas, broad surfaces of the reef flat are covered with a thick carpet of the rubbery green colonial "anemone" *Zoanthus sociatus*. Another characteristic of the reef flat is the sizeable accumulation of sand and pebble-size fragments of reef debris, consisting mostly of coral, miniscule shells, and other skeletal material.

Rear Zone

Beyond the reef flat on the edge of the lagoon is the rear zone. It is the only part of the reef crest subjected to moderate wave energy. Typically the rear zone is quite shallow, with water depths ranging from 0.6 to 9 feet, and consequently, it can be rich in diversity of shallow-water stony corals. Massive boulder corals, brain corals, starlet corals, and the yellow porous corals are quite common.

Barren Zone

On the other margin of the reef crest, seaward of the breaker zone and in slightly deeper water, lies the region that Goreau called the "barren zone." On Caribbean reefs, this area may be called the lower palmata zone. As this name implies, elkhorn coral is abundant here, as are boulder corals, brain corals, lettuce corals, and star corals. The fire corals and spiny black urchins also reside in this zone. Smashed branching corals encrusted with coralline red algae are common. Less than luxuriant stands of elkhorn corals can be dominant to depths of 24 feet.

The name "barren zone" is derived from the barren sand encircling and dividing patch reefs in the zone. The bottom is far from barren, though it does lack large coral heads. It has been suggested that the absence of corals in these barren areas can be attributed to the long-spined black urchin and other grazers that tend to overbrowse the areas within the shelter of the patch reefs.

Back Reef

The typical Caribbean back reef (the area between the reef crest and shore) described by Goreau has two major zones: the inshore zone and the lagoonal zone.

The inshore zone is an area along the shoreline that shows considerable variation. It may consist of a narrow inshore reef, or a zone of algae-covered rubble, or simply coarse calcareous sand.

The lagoonal zone is the shallow water zone (typically 1.5 to more than 45 feet deep) that separates the barrier reef from the shore. The lagoon itself may be several hundred feet to several miles wide and can be divided into four subzones: grass beds, patch reefs, hard grounds, and barren-sediment surfaces.

Inshore Zone

The interface between land and reef is called the inshore zone. Land and the marine environment are inextricably linked, for most of the nutrients that support the growth and development of marine plants and animals comes from the land. Scrub vegetation, mangroves, palms, seagrass beds, and coastal swamps are vital elements in an integrated coral reef community. Collectively, they function as a natural filtering system by trapping and removing tremendous amounts of sediment and nutrients that tend to accumulate in this zone. This process keeps the reef waters free of coral-choking turbidity and nutrients. Still another particularly important role of the inshore zone is to provide a safe nursery for juvenile fish and invertebrates.

Because the zone is subjected to exposure above water as well as intense sunlight with every low tide, it is not a zone that encourages growth of a broad diversity of corals.

The shoreline in the inshore zone is variable within narrow limits, but it is most commonly a sandy beach, algae-covered rocks, or a narrow fringing reef of star corals, brain corals, and algae-covered surfaces.

Lagoonal Zone

The lagoonal environment is commonly a zone that is dominated by sandy bottoms, vast fields of sea grass, scattered patch reefs, clumps of coral, and hard grounds.

Grass Beds: The bottom of the lagoon is often a lush meadow of turtle grass (*Thalassia testudinum*). Climbing species of benthonic foraminifera and other encrusters can be found on grass blades. Look closely between the blades of grass and you will find an array of green algae, rose corals, starlet corals, and fine finger corals protruding between the blades. Here too, *Halimeda* and other calcareous green algae are quite common.

The lagoonal grass beds provide cover and concealment for a rich fauna comprised not only of juvenile fish and invertebrates, but also of an abundance of benthic crustaceans, mollusks, and echinoids. The quiet waters of the lagoon are also home to such diverse organisms as ivory bush coral, fire corals, gorgonians, and sea anemones. Since one of the principal functions of grass beds is to filter nutrients and sediments washed into reef waters from land, coral growth here is further limited by the inevitable turbidity.

Patch Reefs: The patch reefs scattered throughout the lagoon support a rich fauna of stony corals, soft corals, and sponges. The hard corals and algae are typically forms adapted to conditions of low light and suspended sediments as might be found in deeper water on the forereef. Therefore, many deep water corals and algae are present on the lagoonal patch reefs. Slow-growing star corals, brain corals, and plates of lettuce coral are not unusual. *Madracis*, the pencil coral, baffles the fine sediments and can grow upward rapidly. At the same time, the deep-water corals attract other deep-water associates such as clams, worms, "irregular" (burrowing) sea urchins, and brittle stars.

Sand Plains: Where sediments have not been stabilized by algae or grass beds, the bottom may be barren and sediment covered. The apparent bareness is the result of activity of burrowing organisms, especially *Callianassa*, the burrowing shrimp. *Callianassa* builds an impressive cone of sediment over an elaborate maze of tunnels in the substrate. It is not uncommon to see a sandy lagoonal bottom covered with these cones, looking for all the world like a microcosmic mountain range.

Hard Grounds: Where the lagoon floor has been swept clean of accumulating sediments, a hard, rocky bottom may be exposed. These rocky surfaces are covered by a great diversity of algae, soft corals, and encrusting sponge growth. Although these sessile benthos cannot become well established on unstable substrates, they tend to do very well on the hard grounds. The golfball and finger corals

Mustard hill coral growing on hard ground.

are frequently found with diverse associates including shrimp, crabs, anemones, and sea urchins.

Forereef

Nowhere on the reef is the dependence of zonation on water energy and light penetration more clearly demonstrated than on the forereef. Corals in the form of huge mounds or boulders on shallow level bottoms, where sunlight is abundant, grow increasingly outward rather than upward, as depth increases and bottom slope becomes vertical. At a depth of about 80 feet, the coral flattens out until it resembles a platter in order to capture enough sunlight to survive. Thus, coral-growth forms develop in response to diminishing light gradients and changing bottom profiles. Depth, sedimentation, and bottom profile are secondary elements influencing reef zonation.

Forereef profiles around the world vary significantly. Indeed, even on the island of Jamaica, which Goreau used as a model for reef zonation, there is considerable diversity in forereef profiles. To describe a single zonation pattern applicable to reefs around the world would be impossible.

Forereef zonation, on a world-wide basis, can only be described in the most general terms of growth relations because of differing wave energy, water transparency, and nutrient levels. The classic reef zonation commonly used in the Caribbean is, unfortunately, applicable only to the reefs of the Caribbean. However, that forereef zonation is particularly useful in regional studies because a similar geologic history, light and water transparency, wave energy, and reef-dwelling organisms have resulted in similar forereef profiles throughout the Caribbean.

Forereef Profile

The extensive studies conducted on Jamaican reefs by Goreau and his associates have produced the best documented forereef zonation in the Caribbean and perhaps in the world. Seaward of the reef crest, the classic Caribbean reef has been divided into the shallow forereef, the seaward slope, and the deep forereef.

The Shallow Forereef

Mixed Zone: Just seaward of the barren zone on the reef crest, lies the mixed zone, an area of great coral abundance and diversity. This zone is dominated by the massive boulder coral, *Montastrea annularis*. Matching these massive coral heads in abundance are fields of staghorn coral (*Acropora cervicornis*). Here, too, are the castle-like battlements of *Dendrogyra cylindrus*, the pillar coral.

On the gentle slope of the mixed zone (which ranges in depth from 6 to 45 feet) many other corals are conspicuous in their diversity. There are the fragile leaves of lettuce coral (*Agaricia agaricites*) and the hemispherical brain corals

(*Diploria* species and *Meandrina meandrites*). Great boulders of *Siderastrea siderea*, the round starlet coral, are mixed with *Madracis mirabilis*, the pencil coral, and *Porites astreoides*, the mustard hill coral.

There are other corals that are of far less consequence. A few poorly developed elkhorn corals (*Acropora palmata*) and gorgonians grow sparsely, providing scant cover for the anemones, shrimp, and fire worms that live in the mixed zone. Here the green calcareous alga, *Halimeda*, as well as the filamentous algae, are abundant.

Buttress Zone: Perhaps the richest of the reef's coral habitats, the buttress zone or spur-and-groove zone, is characterized by steep coral buttresses that develop in depths of 6 to 60 feet. The buttresses with their vertical sides can range from 9 to 36 feet high and develop at right angles to the reef crest, which tends to parallel the shore. The buttresses appear to grow upward and outward from the shallow reef, in response to the need for sunlight by the corals and the movement of the sea.

In the buttress zone, massive boulder corals, *Montastrea annularis*, are dominant, whereas the buttress walls are festooned with flattened lettuce corals, *Agaricia agaricites*. Along the shallows, the buttresses are crowned with scattered stands of *Eusmilia fastigiata* (flower coral), as well as branching corals and brain corals. The fungus corals, *Mycetophyllia* species, are also common.

Between the buttresses or spurs, narrow surge channels or grooves disperse wave energy and permit sediments, which would otherwise smother the reef, to flow seaward and away from the shallow reef. As the buttresses grow, they frequently roof over the sand channels and, in time, form tunnels. Typically, the movement of the shifting sands is not restricted. It is not uncommon, however, for rapidly growing corals, such as *Acropora cervicornis* (staghorn coral), to spill over onto the surface of a sand channel and completely overgrow its seaward end.

Seaward Slope

Forereef Terrace: Between the buttress zone and the steep slope of the forereef escarpment is the forereef terrace, an intermediate, gently sloping zone (typically in depths from 24 to 60 feet). Sand channels on the forereef terrace tend to be much wider (90 to 300 feet wide) than in the buttress zone, forming sandy plains between broad, parallel lobes of coral growth. The lobes are actually flattened mounds of staghorn coral overgrowing a boulder-coral framework. Unless heavy storms have broken its delicate branches, dense thickets of staghorn coral dominate the forereef terrace of Caribbean reefs. It is known therefore as the cervicornis zone.

Although there are fewer encrusting corals than in the buttress zone, the forereef terrace does have a diversity of coral. Star coral (*Montastrea cavernosa*), cactus coral (*Madracis decactis*), and finger coral (*Porites porites*) are well represented. Other corals commonly found on the forereef terrace are the pencil corals, brain corals, flower corals, and the fungus corals. Common, too, are the sponges, the gorgonians, and the crinoids. Following the massive dieoff of the black spiny sea urchin *Diadema antillarum* in 1983, the fleshy alga *Lobophora*, no longer checked by the urchin's grazing, spread like wildfire across the forereef terrace.

Along the seaward edge of the forereef terrace, the reef forms a low, almost continuous, sill. This sill consists of a band of luxuriant coral growth, about 6 feet high and 21 feet wide.

Forereef Escarpment: Below the sill, the forereef falls away in a long, steep scarp to depths of 75 to 120 feet. The sill at the top of the forereef escarpment tends to restrict the downhill movement of sediment. The more limited the flow is, the steeper the escarpment. In the Caribbean, this area is called the annularis zone. Here the flattened growth forms of the massive boulder coral, *Montastrea annularis*, and plate corals dominate. Sponges and gorgonians thrive on the forereef escarpment as do the pillar, brain, starlet, and finger corals.

Narrow sand channels facilitate the funnelling of sediment down the forereef escarpment. The escarpment ends in a broad sand plain called the moat. In the moat, a rubble pile of coral boulders and staghorn coral tumbled from the face of the escarpment can be found. At the base of this underwater cliff is a notch, which indicates that the escarpment was originally formed as a wave-cut cliff during a period of lower sea levels in the last Ice Age.

Forereef Slope: Angling down gently from the escarpment is a sediment-covered plain called the forereef slope, ranging in depth from 90 to 195 feet. Scattered living corals occur in the moat separating the forereef escarpment from the prominent coral pinnacles of the forereef slope. Along the upper forereef slope, boulder corals are the dominant frame builders. Pinnacles formed by loosely stacked, shingle-like, flattened boulder corals are imposing.

The lower forereef slope is characterized by large, plate-like lettuce and scroll corals (*Agaricia undata*), flattened boulder corals, and sponges. Low, ridge-like pinnacles drop almost vertically on their seaward edges. Soft corals, lettuce corals, fungus corals, pencil corals, flower corals, and *Leptoseris cucullata* (saucer coral) are also common on the lower slope. In addition, solitary corals (*Scolymia* species) as well as the green algae *Penicillus* species and *Halimeda copiosa* and other calcareous algae are common.

Deep Forereef

The Wall: Perhaps the most dramatic aspect of the reef is the deep forereef zone popularly described as "the wall." This nearly vertical escarpment with its slope as great as 80° ranges in depth from 195 to 360 feet. On the irregular face of the wall, gorgonians, sponges, and black corals (antipatharians) dominate. Near the top of the vertical wall, only a few flattened corals are conspicuous because the depth is too great for most reef-building corals. Here, on the reef, the deep-water sclerosponges are dominant. They can grow to a diameter of more than 3 feet and are sufficiently numerous to compete with corals. Other organisms scattered across the upper reaches of the vertical cliff are the calcareous green alga *Halimeda cryptica*, encrusting red algae, hydrozoans, and ahermatypic corals.

Island Slope: Below the wall is a hard, rocky substrate ranging in depth from 360 to 900 feet and deeper. This zone is termed the island slope. Scattered across its cavernous surface are demosponges, ahermatypic corals, crinoids, gorgonians, antipatharians, and reef talus.

Indo-Pacific Reef Profile

The backreef and reef-crest zones of Indo-Pacific reefs are similar to the equivalent zones of Caribbean reefs. However, higher wave energy commonly results in well-developed algal ridges along the seaward margin of Pacific reef crests. In contrast to Caribbean reef zonations, scientific studies of the Indo-Pacific reefs tend to divide the entire outer reef complex into two broad zones: the reef front and the outer slope.

Reef Front

The zonation included in the Indo-Pacific reef front corresponds to the mixed zone, buttress zone, and forereef terrace of Caribbean reefs. Consequently, the shallow reef front has a distinctive zone of coral buttresses divided by sand channels. The bottom of the reef front is typically flat to gently sloping. Because of the abundance of sunlight and water movement, branching and boulder corals proliferate.

The reef front is inhabited by diverse corals from the genera *Acropora* (branching corals), *Porites* (finger corals), and *Pocillopora* (encrusting corals). As the reef profile grows steeper (approaching nearly vertical), the encrusting corals and plate corals become dominant.

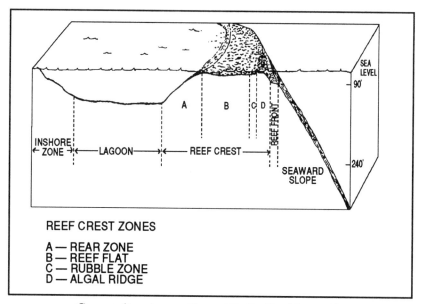

Generalized zonation of Indo-Pacific reefs.

Outer Slope

The outer slope of Indo-Pacific reefs falls away sharply at an angle of 45° or more. It begins in a depth of about 90 feet and continues seaward to a depth of 240 feet. The bottom of the outer slope is covered with crenellated platy corals and layered shingles of plate-like star corals, and button corals.

PATTERNS

Although we tend to emphasize the differences, there are many similarities in coral reef development, wherever reefs grow. Where there are shallow water and abundant sunlight, mounds of boulder, brain, and star corals will grow on level to gently sloping substrates. In protected waters, these corals will typically be overgrown by the faster growing branching corals. However, the development of branching corals may be limited by the destructive wave action of tropical storms. Such violent weather often leaves only a framework of massive corals. Shallow reefs on level or gently sloping bottoms typically develop coral buttresses with intervening surge channels.

As available sunlight dims with depth, vertical reef surfaces, or turbid water, corals tend to flatten to expose more individual polyps to the sunlight. In this manner, the ratio of energy invested to skeletal construction is minimized. Loose layering of flattened, plate corals is consequently typical of coral growth in deep water, or on vertical surfaces. Clearly, reef profile is determined by water depth and bottom slope as they affect reef growth, regardless of location.

Dolphin herd, Bahamas.

West Indian manatee of Florida.

CHAPTER 11

MANKIND AND
THE REEF ECOSYSTEM

It hardly seems possible that just 30 years ago Rachel Carlson wrote, " . . . only within the moment of time represented by the present century has one species - man - acquired significant power to alter the nature of his world." Indeed, in the intervening years, a potentially irreversible threat to the ocean reefs of the world has been steadily developing, and with time running out, the mounting problems appear to be overwhelming us. There has been much public anguish over the environmental poisoning of our oceans, but little in the way of corrective action.

HISTORICAL PERSPECTIVE

The coral reef ecosystem has existed on this planet for more than *200 million years*. In the comparatively short time humans have been on Earth, we have succeeded in fouling our environment, in the process poisoning not only ourselves but, very likely, our descendants. In our rush to exploit the resources of reef and coastal zone, we have - knowingly or unknowingly - posed a serious threat to the continued existence of the coral reefs of the world. And, much of what we have wrought threatens to contaminate all the world's oceans.

MANKIND AND REEF IN HARMONY

One of the oldest relationships between humans and coral reefs dates back an estimated 30,000 years, when aboriginal people drew their sustenance from fish taken from the waters surrounding their South Pacific reefs. Paleolithic burial sites have revealed coral mixed among human remains suggesting that, like the ancient Greeks, the aboriginal fishermen wore coral talismans as a source of immortality, as well as a device to ward off evil.

From that time to the present, the relationship of mankind to the coral reef has evolved steadily from the simple gathering of reef organisms for food and the carving of coral jewelry. Today, the coral reef means big business. The reef provides gifts of food, medicine, clothing, and shelter, but beyond the obvious, there is the ethereal quality . . . the tranquility, the joy, and the inspiration.

The potential of this almost mystical attraction to the sea is not lost on the entrepreneurs and developers. It is suggested that in the Florida Keys alone the coral reefs support an industry worth $100 million annually. As a world-wide industry, the manufacture of jewelry from precious corals generates an estimated $1 billion each year. The coral reefs of the world provide a range of benefits so vast they can scarcely be counted. They are international resources that are not only invaluable, but more importantly, irreplaceable.

Food from the Reef

The coral reefs of the world have traditionally been used as fishing grounds. An estimated 12 percent of the world's fish harvest comes from waters surrounding reef areas. *Properly managed*, the coral reef can provide an endless supply of lobsters, shrimp, crabs, turtles, squid, octopus, fish, snails, and clams. Today, sea cucumbers, urchins, and sea weed are regarded as important food sources and vast tonnages are being harvested in the Pacific.

Another abundant food supply, algae, has for years been a significant source of inexpensive food and food additives. Algae are used in ice cream, and in many coastal areas, salt flats remind us that from the waters of the sea comes salt. Even the very water surrounding the reef is an important food source. Mixed with soy milk, it becomes tofu, a nutritious and vital food in many parts of the world.

Advances in mariculture research are constantly increasing the food yield of underwater farms, and at the same time, high-technology fishing has increased catches beyond traditional limits. Entire cultures, for generations upon generations, have relied on the reef as their sole source of sustenance.

Medicine from the Reef

Many of these same coastal cultures have practiced a highly effective form of folk medicine involving preparations concocted from marine organisms. In the world of modern medicine, many drugs are being developed from the reef's marine life.

Pharmacologists have isolated and identified more than 1,200 compounds that can be used in the treatment of disorders as diverse as multiple sclerosis, rheumatoid arthritis, and AIDS. Prostaglandin, extracted from gorgonians, is used to treat cancer, cardiovascular disease, ulcers, and asthma. Another drug extracted from sea cucumbers is prolonging life and easing pain in some forms of cancer. Perhaps this is the reef's greatest blessing: in countless ways its gifts serve as the catalyst for the production of medicines to end human suffering.

Shelter from the Reef

The coral reef shelters the shore from storms and protects the low-lying coastal zones from erosion. Its coral sands reinforce beaches and low islands. The upper Florida Keys themselves are built on underpinnings of 125,000-year-old fossil reefs.

Without the security of the reef, it is unlikely that many of the world's diverse coastal cultures could have developed. From ancient times, these cultures had a fundamental dependence on the reef. Its coral rocks provided the building stones, tiles, and cement to construct the houses and walls that have sheltered untold generations of coastal dwellers.

Dollars from the Reef

Sailing among the coral atolls of the Pacific in the autumn of 1835, Charles Darwin was nearly overwhelmed by their soul-stirring beauty. This same aesthetic appeal has continued to attract visitors, and with the evolution of the travel industry of the 1900s, tourism has quickly focused on coral reefs.

Remote island countries, unheard of only a few years ago, are celebrated meccas of tourism today. Lovely coral islets on the Great Barrier Reef, which as recently as 1956 were visited by a mere handful of intrepid gogglers or bird-watchers, today are daily stops for swift 500-passenger trimarans.

Off the coast of India lies the low archipelago of the Maldives, an impoverished island nation that in 1972 had but two modest hotels. With its discovery by European sun-worshippers, commerce embraced the Maldives. By 1981, in less than 10 years, the Maldives were home to 37 major resorts. The same extraordinary growth in tourism and consequent development is being experienced by tropical and subtropical islands and coastal zones throughout the world.

Saturation of People

With the encroachment and subsequent activity of humans, coral reefs and coastal zones throughout the world are suffering serious degradation. An estimated 70 percent of the entire population of southeast Asia lives in highly exploited coastal areas. This same pattern holds true in Australia and, for that matter, in most island nations. As populations swell, people encroach more and more on the coastal zones. In Florida alone, an estimated 4,000 new people take up residence on its already people-saturated coasts <u>each week</u>! Along the Gulf Coast of the United States, the population density has increased an amazing 35 percent in the past 10 years.

HUMAN IMPACT ON THE REEF

As coastal areas reel under the impact of the exploding encroachment of mankind, a host of unaddressed problems surfaces. The need for space creates pressures to dredge and fill adjacent mangrove swamps and low coastal areas, destroying in the process not only important wildlife habitats, but also the coral reef.

At the same time humans are cutting and clearing coastal rain forests for future development and altering freshwater flow, they are scarring the hills above the coasts with strip mines.

The disposal of waste frequently results in still more coastal pollution and dumping.

Red mangrove roots under water.

Add to this the very significant problems of wreckage, anchoring, and collecting. Insensitive fishing and diving practices can be equally devastating in their impact on the reef. Each activity affects the delicate balance that maintains the coral reef.

There is no way to remedy decades of neglect and abuse in a few years, but if we are willing to undertake the long-term remedial action necessary for the recovery and protection of the reefs we now exploit, it is vital that we understand the impact of human abuses.

Sediment

To the extent that any alteration of the environment is potentially destructive to the reef ecosystem, increased sedimentation from any source is particularly dangerous. The most luxuriant and diverse coral growth occurs where oceanic waters are clear and clean. When reef waters are loaded with suspended sediments, plankton, and nutrients, the sunlight so vital to the photosynthetic algae is effectively reduced. Once the ability of zooxanthellae to photosynthesize is seriously impaired, these algae either are expelled from the host coral or die, resulting in coral bleaching. The coral will be weakened and its growth rate decreased.

Coastal-land clearing and development are particularly threatening to reef health because these activities generate large amounts of sediments that are eventually carried by runoff to the ocean. Nature, free of human interference, handles these materials easily. Under natural conditions, coral reefs are protected by coastal mangroves and grass beds, which trap sediments washed off land. However, with increased pressure for more coastal development, these natural traps are being destroyed by dredging and filling. As a result, the reef is unprotected from increased sedimentation and turbidity and from the potentially lethal effect of nitrates, phosphates, and hydrogen sulfide released as lime mud is dredged from shallow-water zones.

Whether or not corals can survive sediment accumulation is related to the coral species, as well as to the rate of sedimentation and grain size of the sediment. The size and shape of the coral polyp, the shape of its colony, and the polyp's ability to secrete mucus determine its survivability. Certain polyps, such as those of brain corals, have large tentacles that can effectively throw off even coarse-grained sediment, if it accumulates slowly. Pillar corals shed sediment by virtue of their shapes, whereas other corals, like the deep-pitted star corals, secrete mucus nets to trap and remove sediments.

Although many corals are remarkably resistant to sediment suffocation, other corals have little defense against heavy sedimentation, aside from their shapes and positions on the reef. As the sediment covers these corals, they suffocate and die. If the coral does not die, it will, at the very least, be weakened and more susceptible to bacterial infection (white band disease or black band disease) or algal overgrowth. Accumulating soft sediment may prevent settlement by new coral larvae. In addition, the sediment is likely to contain toxic substances, either leached in or added by runoff or boaters.

The strong correlation between construction, dredging, and filling operations and coral mortality is unequivocal. Perhaps the reefs of the Florida Keys are the best documented example of sedimentation impact on coral reefs. Although people have inhabited the Keys for 2,000 years, it was not until well into the 20th century that they had any significant impact on its reefs.

Between 1905 and 1912, however, the marine environment of the Florida Keys was so radically altered that it was forever changed. During that time, industrialist Henry M. Flagler undertook the construction of the ill-fated Overseas Railroad, a rail system connecting Miami to the island city of Key West. Over 20 million cubic yards of fill material necessary to build embankments were dredged from the shallows along the path of the railroad. Scientific investigation utilizing X-ray imagery has demonstrated a cause-and-effect relationship between construction and reduced growth rate of corals during the period of construction.

With destruction of the railroad by the 1935 hurricane and subsequent conversion of the railway bed to an automobile highway by 1938, land clearing and dredging of coastal zones continued on a massive scale. Coral growth was significantly reduced during this period. Not until filling operations were halted did the corals begin to recover.

Excessive sedimentation of reef waters is a serious concern and is every bit as lethal to the coral reef environment as is the use of dynamite to loosen coral heads.

Poisoning of the Reefs

Throughout the history of mankind, oceans have been a preferred site for waste disposal. What began innocently with the disposal of natural wastes, easily digested by the environment, has grown into a nightmare of highly toxic synthetic materials that now threatens all environments throughout the world.

Ocean dumping of sludge and other waste was to end in 1981 according to the Ocean Dumping Act of 1977, yet dumping continues. Indiscriminate disposal of sewage, fertilizers, pesticides, herbicides, and industrial wastes has caused environmentalists to call our coastal waters a "stew of poisons." Coral reefs throughout the world are endangered because of high nutrient levels, sediment contamination, chlorine, toxic metals, and attendant turbidity.

Swimming in Sewage

Beach on Guam.

Many coastal cities, including the sunbelt cities of Miami and Key West, openly discharge sewage within 1 mile of tourist swimming beaches. What a treat - to discover one had been swimming in sewage! In other coastal regions, poorly designed septic systems release nutrient-rich waste into porous limestone through which it percolates and emerges almost unaltered into the sea water. This phenomenon is happening in reef zones throughout the world.

In the United States alone, more than 2,000 municipal and industrial treatment plants discharge wastes into the country's waters. Heavy metals and toxins such as lead, mercury, chromium, cobalt, and zinc, found in the bottom sediment of Florida Bay and John Pennekamp Coral Reef State Park, have reached levels of environmental concern.

Strange Sounding Names

Today more than 66,000 chemicals are in daily use in the United States and almost all of them are potentially dangerous. The annual by-product of United States industrial muscle is approximately *300 million tons of toxic wastes*, much of which is discharged directly into our oceans. Although the scale may vary, the same holds true for every other country in the world.

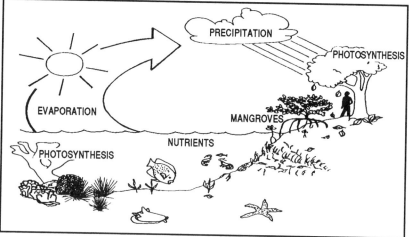

Nutrient cycle.

Fertilizers release high levels of nutrients including nitrates and phosphates into coastal waters. High-nutrient loading from fertilizers or sewage can trigger algal blooms, which deplete the reef's oxygen and kill marine organisms.

Eutrophication, a significant increase in algal and bacterial growth common in polluted areas, is strong evidence of discharge of sewage and industrial and agricultural wastes. Every day high levels of mysterious and deadly carcinogens such as PCB, DDT, dioxin, and vinyl chloride seep into our land, our potable water supply, and the sea. Even trace amounts of DDT and PCB (common in

Kelthane and *Lindane* and other pesticides used on sugar cane) are bioconcentrated in higher organisms of the food web, eventually consumed by humans. Dioxin itself is so unspeakably virulent a poison that a mere drop diluted in 10,000 gallons of water is considered to be a deadly concentration.

Burial at Sea

Down through the ages, we have used the ocean as a vast garbage can into which we could throw all our refuse. The contemptuousness of our "out of sight, out of mind" attitude was perhaps forgivable in the past when we may have been ignorant of the consequences, but today, we must be held accountable. The curse of our unchecked dumping surely will be visited on future generations, as certainly as it is on the present generation.

Plastics at Sea

The important AN-NEX V law prohibits the dumping of plastic debris by ships at sea; but the United States Navy, by its own admission, dumps 4 tons of plastics in the ocean *every day*. The shipping industry is responsible for an estimated 6.6 million tons of

Garbage on Red Sea coral reef.

oceanic trash annually. A high percentage of this debris (about 550 thousand tons) is in the form of plastic containers.

All over the world, the ocean surface is fouled by bloated bodies of sea creatures killed by plastics and other nonbiodegradables. An endangered sea turtle mistakes a plastic bag for the jellyfish it normally eats. The plastic clogs its intestines and the poor creature dies. A damaged polypropylene fish net is abandoned by uncaring fishermen and a bottle-nosed dolphin is snared and drowns. Sea birds are trapped and strangled in plastic six-pack yokes or monofilament fishing lines. Ocean fish searching for food swallow bobbing styrofoam pellets and die. Plastic garbage bags discarded by ships, small craft, and oil rigs drift onto coral reefs, then wrap tightly around branching corals, killing them.

At What Cost?

On a popular Pacific island, the commander of a United States military installation admits during a press conference that the military has been disposing of active chemical and biological war materials for years by burying them. He does not admit to burying nuclear materials. The geologist in the gathering thinks about the island's porous limestone underpinnings and then sighs. The islands of the Pacific know about nuclear testing as well; radioactivity has found its way into their food chain.

The disposal of garbage and human wastes is not confined to the military and the ocean-shipping industry. Although many coastal nations and developed countries deal effectively with wastes in properly lined, sealed, and buried land fills, others, including the Philippines and Saipan, use the simple expedient of bull-dozing their garbage into the sea. Many third world countries are pressured by rich industrialized nations to accept barges loaded with municipal wastes, proving that it is infinitely easier to exploit a poor country's need for cash than to admit their own unwillingness to clean up after themselves.

More Power to You

Thermal pollution is yet another area of concern to reef investigators. Electric generating plants and desalination plants are but two thermal energy sources whose pollution can be harmful to coral reefs.

Extreme temperature fluctuations result from the circulation of water to cool the generating plants. With a water temperature increase of as little as 5° F, hermatypic corals will expel their vital zooxanthellae. Because tropical organisms commonly live near their upper temperature tolerances, temperature shifts of as little as 4 to 6° F substantially reduce the number and variety of organisms living in the reef ecosystem.

In addition, many desalination plants have a record of polluting neighboring waters with hypersaline effluents, antifouling chemicals, copper, zinc, nickel, and other heavy metals. With the everpresent threat of oil spills and radiated coolants contaminating the waters contiguous to the plants, still another environmental threat hangs over the coral reef.

Oil and Gas Production

Day-to-day pollution of coral reef ecosystems by the release of hydrocarbons occurs with boating, bilge pumping, deck flushing, and natural oil seeps; but it is exploration, production, and transport of petroleum products that carries the risk of dramatic environmental damage. More than 1,000 patented chemicals have been used to facilitate hydrocarbon drilling and production. Although the impact of most of these chemicals on the coral reef community is unknown, it is unlikely that delicate coral polyps would thrive under a constant bath of caustic acids, bactericides, dispersants, and other drilling fluids.

As the pace of leasing, drilling, and production increases in the shallow reef zones throughout the world's oceans, the threat of extensive reef damage grows ever greater. With increased production comes a corresponding expansion in tanker and supertanker traffic and greater potential for catastrophic environmental disaster.

Another problem associated with hydrocarbon production is increased sedimentation generated by off-shore drilling. The discharge of toxic drilling muds and cuttings also can contribute to mortality of coral and other marine organisms. The impact of both of these disturbances on the marine environment can be mitigated by using proper drilling procedures.

As demonstrated by the 1986 Panama spill, oil pollution affects corals directly by damaging tissue and by obstructing coral metabolism. The result is a significant slow-down in feeding, respiration, recruitment, reproduction, and growth.

Hydrocarbons are released into the marine environment during production and by accidents such as the rupture of a storage tank on the Caribbean coast of Panama, the blowout of the Union Rincon platform off Santa Barbara and the Ixtoc I platform in the Gulf of Mexico, the founderings of the *Argo Merchant* off Nantucket and the Exxon *Valdez* off Alaska, and terrorist acts like those of the Persian Gulf War. In addition, every day dangerous levels of hydrocarbons are dumped into reef and coastal zone waters by indiscriminate platform hosings and tankers flushing out ballast tanks.

Effluent discharge and untreated stormwater runoff greatly increase the number of bacteria and algae in reef waters, substantially reducing the level of dissolved oxygen. Corals covered by hydrocarbons secrete mucus nets, pulsate, and use ciliary water movement to throw off the threatening material.

Recent research suggests that the lighter fraction of petroleum, which mixes with sea water, is more damaging to corals and bottom organisms than the heavy fraction, which floats on the surface. Of course, the heavy hydrocarbons drift to shore and destroy the shore birds and other life forms on land.

Oil slicks cause an initial increase in bacteria and algae in the water, decrease sunlight, and reduce dissolved oxygen. Eventually, bacterial decay and the sun's ultraviolet rays will degrade the hydrocarbons, but probably not before the damage is done.

For these reasons, countries like the United States have proposed federal controls to limit the impact of oil production on *live-bottom* areas. Concern about the prospect of oil spills caused the Great Barrier Reef Marine Park Authority to prohibit all oil and gas production activities in and around the waters of the Great Barrier Reef. Similar concerns in the United States led to the designation of the

Florida Keys National Marine Sanctuary in November 1990. However, this did nothing to reduce the threat of hydrocarbons related to boating and shipping activity.

Shipwrecks

Every day, somewhere in the world, a vessel runs aground or sinks in the waters surrounding a coral reef. Nowhere are shipwrecks and boat groundings better documented than in Florida's Key Largo National Marine Sanctuary. In the recent past, numerous vessels have run aground on its reefs . . . and a few have sunk. During 1986 alone, 40 groundings were bad enough to be reported, and nobody knows how many went unreported. Boulder corals with enormous gouges still carrying slashes of bottom paint bear silent witness to their numbers.

Molasses Reef, a Favorite Target

Molasses Reef, a popular scuba diving and snorkeling site in the Key Largo National Marine Sanctuary, has had a long history of shipwrecks. Interestingly, the fact that it has been marked with a lighted tower for years has not deterred really determined wreckers.

In February 1973, for example, the *Ice Fog*, a 70-foot tugboat, sank in 130 feet of water. The barge it had under tow ran hard aground on Molasses Reef. The barge, coincidentally, was loaded with molasses as was the first ship wrecked on that ill-starred reef. Months after the grounding, divers were still surfacing from dives there coated with a gooey, black film.

The next major wreck at Molasses Reef occurred in May of 1977. A tanker went aground on the reef and took several days to be refloated.

The *Wellwood*

Perhaps the best documented grounding in history also involved Molasses Reef. Early in the morning on

August 4, 1984, the *Wellwood*, a Cypriot grain freighter, ran hard aground during a rain squall. The grounding was unusual in that the freighter had been north-bound, enroute from New Orleans to Europe, carrying a full load of grain. She was using a satellite navigation system instead of taking depth soundings near the reef.

The Wellwood *on Molasses Reef.*

This resulted in the *Wellwood* venturing much closer to the reef than the normal Gulf Stream shipping lanes allowed. She grounded in water 19 to 25 feet deep and sat on the reef for 12 days.

Working together, the Florida Department of Natural Resources, the National Oceanic and Atmospheric Administration, and the U.S. Coast Guard, and the U.S. Geological Survey, along with commercial salvors removed tons of cargo, ballast, and fuel from the grounded ship. On August 16th, she was floated off the reef.

Throughout the entire process, efforts were underway to save the reef and document the destruction. Thousands of square yards of reef had been damaged by the grounding and subsequent salvage operations. Branching elkhorn corals were crushed flat and Molasses Reef's celebrated boulders of star coral were overturned, broken, and abraded. Corals not destroyed by the grounding or salvage, were bleached because the *Wellwood* blocked the sunlight for the 12 days it sat on the reef. Corals and other reef organisms were further damaged by the enormous silt clouds produced by the freighter's prop wash and breakage by the towing cables.

Where the damage was heaviest, over 90 percent of the head corals and 98 percent of the gorgonians were destroyed. Through the days of the ordeal, agency divers worked to mitigate the damage. Broken corals were righted and recemented. Assuming no further groundings, the best estimate of recovery time for the affected area of Molasses Reef is from 12 to 27 years.

During the grounding, continuous efforts were under way to document the impact on the reef environment. In precedent-setting litigation, the National Oceanic and Atmospheric Administration sued the *Wellwood's* owners for $50,000 per day for each of the 12 days the ship was on the reef, and $22 million in civil damages. The state of Florida also sued for damages in the amount of $15 million. The landmark settlement awarded the federal government $6.3 million in compensation for damage to the sanctuary.

Molasses Reef Not an Isolated Case

Other reefs have been at least as badly damaged by ships, though the effects are not nearly so well documented. During a recent stay at the Discovery Bay Marine Laboratory in Jamaica, researchers watched helplessly as an ore carrier, loaded to its Plimsoll marks with bauxite, ran hard aground on the reef crest and forereef. The damage resulting from physical breakage of the corals by the ship was exceeded by that caused by sediment plumes from prop wash and breakage by towing cables.

Bauxite ore carrier on reef at Discovery Bay, Jamaica.

Less dramatic groundings are commonplace as small vessels run aground or are stranded by low tides. Beyond the obvious impact damage, antifouling paint, fuel leaking into the water from the bilges or ruptured fuel tanks, and boat sewage discharged onto the reef are serious causes of coral mortality.

In the Looe Key Marine Sanctuary, for example, a 110-foot catamaran went aground for 18 days. The sewage, garbage, engine oil, and general debris the boat dumped on the reef caused coral damage to more than 3,717 square feet of reef. It is interesting to note that, although required by law, very few of the large "live aboard" boats have adequate containment systems for their sewage.

It has been suggested that most coral damage caused by boats is unintentional and more a result of ignorance than malice. Nevertheless, thoughtless boat operation by unskilled, untrained persons has caused widespread destruction and damage to corals, and poor boat handling implies a dangerously casual attitude about a fragile ecosystem. To prevent damage to reef areas, all boaters should operate their boats slowly and attentively, particularly around shallow corals. All prudent boat operators should familiarize themselves with the surface indications of shallow-reef formations, learn where and how to anchor, and refer to appropriate navigational charts.

Anchor Damage

At first glance, it would seem that, compared to the devastation of a reef by the grounding of a large ship, anchor damage would hardly be worth mentioning. The fact is anchor damage is probably the most common and obvious effect of human activity on the reef, and all vessels are equally guilty, whether the boats of sports fishermen, research ships, or tankers. Typically, the bigger the vessel is, the bigger the anchor, and the bigger the anchor, the greater the likelihood of extensive damage.

When an anchor is dropped directly on a coral formation, the corals commonly are crushed and destroyed by the impact. They can be slashed and uprooted as the anchor's chain or rope drags across the reef while the boat rides at anchor, and even more damage is done when the anchor is recovered. The damage may appear as a deep gouge, triangular scar, overturned coral head, or uprooted sponge or soft coral. (One busy charter-boat captain suggested that large sponges make ideal anchorages; when an anchor is hung up, all he has to do is pull up the sponge!)

Although an abraded or gouged coral surface may not seem to constitute major damage, such seemingly superficial damage can become readily infected by bacteria and algae. Infection that begins on one small scar eventually may destroy an entire coral colony.

Large anchors dragged across a coral reef may leave a trail of destruction 50 feet wide and hundreds of feet long. Conversely, popular scuba diving sites attract thousands of small boats the year around. Molasses Reef, for example, is visited by an estimated 15,000 boats each year. The damage inflicted on such a reef can be mind-boggling.

The installation of permanent moorings at popular diving and fishing sites on reefs around the world has reduced the physical damage of anchoring. Despite concerns that reefs might be more stressed as divers and fishermen flock to the buoyed areas, the addition of the permanent anchoring sites in the Florida Keys sanctuaries has resulted in a significant reduction in anchor damage.

There is no question but that the most popular, and therefore, the most set upon, coral reefs should be equipped with permanent mooring buoys, and anchoring at other sites should be prohibited. In areas where there are no mooring buoys to tie to, boaters should anchor in a sand channel, well away from the reef, using an anchor that will hold fast in the sand. They should check the set of the anchor to insure that it will not drag and that the anchor chain or line does not contact coral. The installation of mooring buoys is one of the most successful methods of reducing direct damage to the coral reef. However, not all reef damage is as easily mitigated. In some cases, damage results from traditional means of gathering food.

Fishing

For centuries, generations of fishermen have harvested the bounty of the coral reef. In third world countries alone, more than 15 million fishermen depend on reefs as their principal source of fish. In most of these same countries, in spite of modern fishing technology, mariculture, artificial reefs, and marine resource management, fishing techniques have changed little over the centuries.

Damage to the coral reef takes many forms. Dragging nets, and the dropping and hauling of fish, crab, and lobster traps, frequently abrades, overturns or breaks corals and destroys other marine organisms. In addition, commercial fishing vessels commonly discard badly damaged nets or traps overboard. Nets snagged on coral reefs are

Net fishing, mainland China.

similarly abandoned. Reef ledges and coral heads are commonly festooned with hooks and lines.

In the old days, although the problem was bad enough, there was the comfort of knowing the traps, nets, and lines would rot eventually and fall away from the reef. Today's fishermen, however, use nondegradable polypropylene nets and monofilament line. Abandoned nets, like abandoned fish traps, continue to trap and kill marine life unless they are found and destroyed.

Destructive Techniques

Along with advances in technology and development of more durable nondegradable materials for fish nets and traps have come new techniques that pose a serious threat to the coral reef ecosystem. So-called *dynamite fishing* takes place daily on reefs all over the world. In Truk Lagoon, intrepid fishermen obtain their explosives from very unstable Japanese ordnance removed from World War II shipwrecks. One philosophical Trukese advised that this fact accounts for the large number of one-armed fishermen on Truk.

Sadly, Cousteau's early experiments showed that the shock wave propagated by the explosion from dynamite fishing ruptured the air bladders of over 90 percent of the fish in the stun radius. Fewer than 10 percent of the fish killed float to the surface to be harvested. The rest are left to rot on the bottom, and the damage to the fish population and the reef ecosystem is incalculable.

Spearfishing is justifiably criticized, particularly when it involves the use of scuba equipment. It allows the fishermen to go deeper and to stay down longer so as to harvest selectively the larger fish and predators that maintain the balance of the reef community.

Fishing the Silent Reefs

After years of non-selective harvesting of anything that swims, fishermen in many developing countries are being forced to use smaller and smaller mesh sizes in their fish nets and traps. In countries such as Jamaica, where fish populations are already severely limited because of low- nutrient supply, the impact of these practices is particularly obvious.

In other countries fishermen have learned to harvest low-density fish populations. Philippine and Japanese fishermen have developed "herding" techniques to gather and drive fish into their nets. One of the most destructive tech-

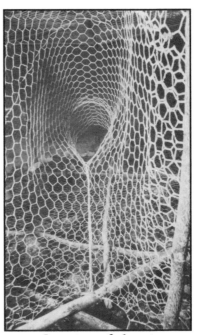

Jamaican fish pot.

niques practiced by fishermen is the use of lines tied to rocks that are heavy enough to crush corals. These rocks are repeatedly dropped on the reef to drive fish out of the coral and into nets.

As fish populations world-wide are steadily reduced by indiscriminate fishing methods, the problem is further complicated by the ongoing destruction of coastal nurseries (seagrass beds and mangrove swamps), where juvenile fish would normally develop. The costs of coastal development grow ever higher. Are we willing to exploit our natural resources regardless of the cost?

The dilemma is how to minimize damage to the coral reef ecosystem without interfering with the fisherman's right to survive and feed his family. The key lies in educating fishermen and demonstrating the benefits of alternatives like offshore fishing and using larger mesh sizes for fish traps, not in outlawing fishing.

Lobster Collecting

The harvesting of spiny lobster, conch, and other shellfish is centered around coral reefs throughout the world. Being omnivorous, nocturnal feeders, lobsters are quite mobile under the cover of darkness. As little as 20 years ago, lobsters were available in great abundance throughout the waters of the Florida Keys and commercial lobster divers boasted of "pulling" 400 pounds of lobsters per day! In fact, lobsters were being removed faster than they could be replaced on the reef, and it eventually became necessary to enact legislation regarding the size, number, and season during which lobsters could be caught.

However, illegal collecting of lobsters goes on daily, despite stiff penalties, fines, and in extreme cases, jail sentences. Poachers are commonly caught collecting lobsters out of season, with catches exceeding legal limits, or taking "shorts" (under-size lobster) and females with eggs.

Even when laws are obeyed, physical damage to the coral reef occurs when commercial lobster traps are carelessly dropped or recovered. In addition to physical damage to the reef, there is the problem of abandoned traps. In the past, lobster "pots" (traps) were constructed of degradable materials, and, if lost underwater, they soon decayed and fell apart. Today, traps are made of plastic or treated wood that does not decay in the marine environment. Consequently, lost or abandoned traps continue to capture lobsters which starve and die, attracting other animals in turn into the fatal traps. Perhaps the answer may lie in a return to degradable materials to prevent unnecessary lobster kills.

Traps are not the only source of physical damage to the reef. In the Keys, greedy divers commonly tip over and damage large boulder corals in search of lobsters.

Among the most senseless acts is the use of noxious chemicals to collect lobster. Divers who are too slow to hand catch lobster (witness the high percentage of lobsters on any reef missing one or both antennae) have found a way to harvest lobster. Someone discovered that lobster can be driven out into the open by squirting chlorine bleach into the recesses of the reef. Although it may have the desired result, it is not without cost. Sessile organisms such as the corals that cannot escape the chemicals die. The use of chemicals must be banned if the senseless destruction of the coral reef ecosystem is to be prevented.

The lobster, like every other organism in the reef environment, has an important role in the fragile balance of life on the reef. Eliminate it and the reef's food web will be seriously altered. This is true of other reef dwellers as well.

Collecting Marine Specimens

Collecting marine specimens varies from institutional research collections, to hobby collectors, to high-volume commercial ventures. Such commercial ventures have become a major industry. For example in Florida alone, the Florida Department of Natural Resources estimates that the value of commercial collection of fish, invertebrates and "live rocks" in state waters exceeds $1 million annually.

Commonly the quickest and easiest way to extract a reef organism may not be the best for the reef. Physical damage may be done to the reef by commercial, amateur, and scientific collectors who break corals to remove reef organisms or "live-rock" substrates.

The taking of live specimens for marine aquaria also is accomplished by using noxious chemicals ranging from *quinaldine* to *sodium hypochlorite* (common laundry bleach) to drive the fish and other motile organisms out of the reef to facilitate collecting. The impact of such toxic substances on delicate coral polyps and most other marine organisms is sudden, dramatic, and often, fatal. Although the practitioners deny it, the fact is that the sessile animals that cannot move and the cryptic (cavity dwelling) animals are commonly so stressed by chemicals they die.

Throughout the Indo-Pacific, particularly in the Philippines, divers supply the aquarium industry with fish caught using sodium cyanide or muro-ami. In addition to the sale of live reef dwellers, there is also a market for bleached coral skeletons. When people are struggling to eke out a meager existence from coastal resources, they cannot understand lectures on resource management.

Collecting Corals and Shells

Throughout the Caribbean and Central America, reef corals are harvested and sold to tourists as jewelry or souvenirs. With each coral sold, the reef is changed, and yet the impact of these entrepreneurs is small when compared to that of commercial collectors. The ornamental-shell and coral industry processes thousands of tons of corals and shells each year, and estimates place the worth of the industry at $1 billion annually.

To assess the impact of commercial collection on the reefs of the world, consider these statistics. In the Philippines alone, in 1 year more than 4,000 tons of shells and 7,000 tons of coral were removed from the reef. In Sri Lanka, coral is mined by the ton and loaded into freighters for foreign marketplaces. In Hawaii, tons of corals are harvested by entrepreneurs using deep-diving submersibles.

Most reef scientists agree that if the reefs are to be preserved the collection of corals must be banned. In the continental United States between 1964 and 1973, prior to legislation banning collection, an estimated *1,560 tons* of elkhorn, staghorn, brain, and pillar corals were taken from Key West reefs by *12* commercial collectors. As the United States law now stands, no corals - living or dead - may be collected from areas on the continental shelf outside the 3-mile limit. Since the State of Florida prohibits collection from the high-tide line to the 3-mile limit, collecting of corals is prohibited on virtually all Florida reefs.

There is little room for optimism because of legislation, for at the same time, the market for coral specimens has grown steadily. The harvesting of corals in reef areas such as the Philippines has increased accordingly. Illegal coral collecting is rampant on reefs around the world.

Everyone acknowledges that coral reefs are an extraordinary resource and those who must have a souvenir are encouraged to photograph the reef and its colorful residents. "Take only pictures, leave only bubbles!" The moral question is: will the desire to collect, to possess, to own a part of the coral reef supersede the desire to preserve the coral reef environment? Is the reef only here to serve at the pleasure of the present generation? What of the generations to come? Who speaks for them?

Tourism and Sport Diving

It has been suggested that there are too many people, and too few reefs. To preserve this most complex of all ecosystems, we must educate those who have it within their grasp to save the coral reefs. The best way to learn about this extraordinary three-dimensional world is to visit

Maldives dive guide feeding moray eel.

it, but can the reefs of the world survive this level of visitation? Those determined to save the reefs are equally determined to preserve individual rights to enjoy the endless bounty of the reef. They are in the humanist/environmentalists' worst kind of "Catch 22."

Everywhere in the world, coral reefs are deteriorating at an alarming rate. There no longer is any question that sport diving, both snorkeling and scuba diving, has had a significant impact on the coral reef ecosystem. The Key Largo National Marine Sanctuary and John Pennekamp Coral Reef State Park are, at the time of this writing, being visited by more than 1.5 million people each year. Many of these visitors will come into direct contact with the corals within the sanctuary. The total effect of human contact on the coral is, at this point, unknown, because it is difficult to separate coral damage by human contact from other causes. It is doubtful that the bumps, abrasions, and the inadvertent removal of the coral's protective mucus that accompany each touch can be beneficial to the coral animal.

Reef Walkers

On the Great Barrier Reef, "reef walking" is a popular tourist activity. On a "reef walk" visitors to the reef actually stroll across the tops of coral colonies at low tide. Entrepreneurs have even designed and marketed thick-soled "reef booties" to protect the tourists' feet from sharp coral.

Considerable time and energy are spent briefing and safe-guarding the visitors from missteps that might cause a tourist to break through the coral. There is considerable concern for the visitor's comfort and safety. Regrettably, there is little concern left over for the coral polyps.

Yellow Submarines

The economic impact of the reef has not been lost on investors. All over the world today, doctors, lawyers, bankers and others are discovering that investment in reef-related tourism is good business, and not nearly as risky as it once was.

In coral reef areas around the world, submersibles are loading tourists and descending to the bottom of the sea for first-hand viewing from the dry, air-conditioned comfort of 50-passenger submarines. Although these vehicles bring the non-diver close to the reef, the impact of 4 or 5 submersible dives a day, 365 days a year,

Nekton gamma submersible, Lee Stocking Island, Bahamas.

can only be guessed. This much is certain: in limited visibility, the submersibles have to maneuver close enough to touch the reef, and they do. And, when a vehicle the size of a Greyhound bus collides with a reef, it is not difficult to imagine the trail of coral rubble it will leave in its wake.

Diver Damage

Sport diving has become a major recreational industry. One Australian scuba school trains and certifies over 500 new ocean divers every week, 52 weeks each year. In the United States, the diving equipment manufacturers have a short-term goal of training and certifying one million sport divers each year. In terms of sheer numbers, it is clear that sport diving has had and will continue to have a dramatic impact on coral reefs around the world. According to statistics from SKINDIVER magazine, if every diver visiting Caribbean reefs causes only *one incident* of reef damage each year, more than one-half million living coral colonies will die.

Currently, the people snorkeling and scuba diving the reefs of the world each year number in the millions. They are typically on vacation and many are diving on the reef with little or no training or experience in coral reef diving. An estimated 75 percent of all divers pays to dive from commercial dive boats. In most diving operations around the world, the operators are prudent enough to check the diver's qualifications. Regrettably, they rarely have taken the time to discuss damage caused by uninformed and careless diving techniques.

The Causes

Much of the physical damage to the reef caused by snorkelers and scuba divers is the result of poor buoyancy control, lack of reef awareness, or, in some cases, the collecting of marine organisms. Often new reef divers, in addition to being untrained for the environment, are overweighted and using unfamiliar equipment. When tossed about in the surge, they steady themselves by grabbing what appears to be a hard, inanimate handhold.

Importance of buoyancy control for divers.

Poor swimmers find they can rest and get their heads above water at the same time by sitting or standing on a convenient coral head, breaking delicate coral branches and damaging tissue of boulder corals. Even resting on a sand bottom may result in destruction of young coral polyps. Underwater photographers may become so engrossed in taking pictures that they are unaware when they bump or break a delicate coral. Some scuba divers grab, hold, and pull on corals to drag themselves along the bottom. Their rationale is that they are conserving air or fighting a current.

These are not the wanton acts of irresponsible, insensitive people. For the most part, unless someone informs them, they're not even aware of their impact. It is axiomatic that as the number of diving tourists increases, the damage to the reef will increase geometrically.

The Immediate Solution

Is there an answer? From the standpoint of diver-impact, the answer is an unqualified yes. First, informed and enlightened divers are sensitive to the health and well-being of the coral reef environment. Any recreational diver who wants to continue to enjoy diving on coral reefs is going to have to learn to be an environmentalist. There is an increasing awareness among most dive shops, dive boat operators, and training agencies that growth of their industry depends on the health of the coral reefs and careless diving jeopardizes their own livelihoods. This has led many sensitive dive operations to instruct divers and enforce reef diving guidelines themselves. Only enlightened divers, however, can preserve and protect corals from needless damage and death, and the level of education available to inform and enlighten these divers falls well short of the mark.

For example, rather than educate new divers not to handle corals and other marine animals, some entrepreneurs sell them "reef gloves." Gloves commonly encourage divers to hold onto the reef and probably do much more damage than good. To their credit, many dive operations now ban the use of such gloves.

Divers can help slow the damage by boycotting dive operations that violate rules and regulations. Furthermore, every diver can benefit from training offered by diver training agencies in the field of coral reef ecology.

Dive tour operators must instruct first-time reef divers in new scuba skills *before* they enter the water. Dive boat operators can work together to limit diver impact by spreading diving activity over larger areas. With the increasing number of snorkelers and scuba divers wanting to dive the reefs, park and sanctuary interpretive specialists could provide prerequisite briefings for new divers. Such briefings would address the impact of human activity and describe common sense behavior necessary to protect reefs from senseless, thoughtless acts of destruction. Every sport diver will be helping to preserve the coral reef immeasurably if he or she follows these simple guidelines for reef diving

1) Learn to move with finesse around the reef. Fins, dangling hoses, or careless movements break corals; they need to be controlled.

2) Control your buoyancy. All divers (snorkelers or scuba divers) should wear a buoyancy compensator and be proficient in its use. No comfortable diver should need to have a handhold on the coral to steady himself. If you must rest, find a barren, sandy spot on the bottom.

3) Properly weight yourself. The most experienced divers are those with the minimum amount of weight on their belts.

4) Avoid use of reef gloves, knee pads, or other body protection to touch marine organisms that shouldn't be touched.

5) Avoid standing, kneeling, or sitting on the coral formations. Do not grab or hold on to corals.

6) Avoid destroying spiny sea urchins. They play a vital role in nature's scheme of checks and balances. When urchin populations are reduced, the algae can overgrow and shade the corals.

7) Avoid feeding fish. Fish feeding disrupts natural feeding habits by introducing unnatural food and may result in bodily harm to the diver.

Once divers become sensitized to the fact that corals are living animals, their attitude toward the reef is changed forever. Perhaps the greatest joy of diving on a reef is to discover that wondrous microcosm of life. More than one seasoned diver has been heard to say " . . . that's a whole new world down there."

Divers must become aware of the fragile nature of coral tissue and the need to avoid coral damage. When a coral is broken or badly abraded, the bare wound - much like a wound in human tissue - is vulnerable to bacterial or algal infection. Such diseases can spread over an entire coral colony, eventually killing all of the coral polyps. Even if the coral survives, it will inevitably be scarred and weakened. Typically, energy that would ordinarily be expended in reproduction and growth is used instead for mere survival. The result is a weak, unhealthy, and vulnerable coral colony. The best policy is for divers to avoid any contact that might cause breakage or abrasions to corals.

Kill the Urchin, Kill the Coral

Often, simple acts can do much harm. In the past, one could visit any popular reef dive site and find at least one diver chopping up a long-spined black sea urchin. The diver would be surrounded by clouds of colorful fish feeding on the urchin. The act seemed harmless enough and was certainly good for underwater photography. Unfortunately, killing urchins was very bad for the reef.

The spiny urchin, *Diadema antillarum*, is an algae-grazer that plays a vital role in maintaining the biologic balance of the reef ecosystem. Eliminate the spiny sea urchin, which almost happened after the mysterious urchin dieoff of 1983, and the unchecked algae will overgrow the corals. The benthic marine herbivore plays an important role in the continuing health of the coral reef ecosystem. By the simple elimination of one element in the community, the health of the entire coral reef ecosystem is threatened.

People, A Positive Conservative Force

All the problems associated with human impact can be mitigated through education and the process of sensitizing people to the fragile nature of the reef community. When people understand that coral polyps are living animals and that the entire balance of the coral reef ecosystem can be endangered by thoughtless acts, they will want to be part of a positive conservative force fighting the waste and abuse of our coral reefs.

Divers ascending from Andros reef.

**REMOVE NOTHING FROM THE REEF
EXCEPT
NOURISHMENT FOR THE SOUL,
CONSOLATION FOR THE HEART,
INSPIRATION FOR THE MIND.**

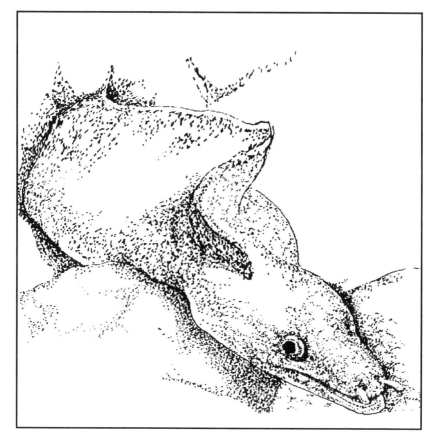

Moray eel.

CHAPTER 12

CAN THE CORAL REEFS BE SAVED?

The deterioration of coral reefs around the world is obvious to any scientist or diver who has returned to visit a familiar reef. Long-term studies are not necessary to make this determination; the rapidity of the decline is alarming. There can no longer be any question. Magazines and newspapers are filled with the distressing facts. Coral bleaching, algal growth, and reef death are becoming all too common.

Turtle over shallow reef.

One reef scientist who has continuously monitored reef vitality since the 1950s suggests, at the present rate of decline, many of Florida's coral reefs will be dead by the year 2009. It's not as though we didn't have fair warning. Long ago, Jacques Cousteau cautioned, " . . . it takes tens of hundreds of years for a living reef to grow, and a very few to render it lifeless." We are living on a planet under siege. World-wide concern over environmental issues is at an all time high, as well it should be. The degradation of the environment has ominous implications for the entire planet.

NATURAL DISASTERS

Mankind has little control over nature's impact on the reef. Hurricanes and storms cause destruction regardless of our insignificant efforts. Over millions of years, coral reefs have been devastated by one spectacular natural disaster after another. The reefs of the Florida Keys alone have survived more than 800 hurricanes in the past 6,000 years. Yet, despite the awesome ripping, crushing, and breaking of corals, these reefs have managed not only to survive these disasters but to thrive. In fact, many branching corals actually propagate new colonies through such breakage while storm waves scour algae and fine sediment from the reef. Nevertheless, negative impact manifests itself in many ways.

Sea level continues to rise. As it rises, coastal lands are flooded, releasing more nutrients into reef waters, which allow more algae to cover reef surfaces. Grazing and boring organisms continue to rasp away on the coral reefs. This is part of nature's ongoing process of life and death. Because resilient coral reefs can survive even the most devastating natural disaster, it is clear that left to themselves and given enough time to recuperate, *the reefs can regain* their vitality. But when reef mortality is caused by human impact, there is no option but to eliminate the stress and give the reefs time to recover.

THE CAUSE OF REEF DETERIORATION

The cause of the present deterioration of coral reefs cannot be attributed to any natural disaster; it can only be traced to human activity. Thoughtless human acts probably do more permanent damage to a reef in one year, than a millennium of natural disasters. Human nature has been to exploit the environment for immediate return, regardless of long-term effects. Wherever in the world impoverished peoples exploit the resources of a coral reef to survive, the degradation of the reef is measurable. Catastrophic oil spills and other environmental disasters, destruction of irreplaceable natural resources like the world's rain forests, which accompany our quest for additional resources, should be of deepening concern to all mankind.

Direct stress on the reef comes from many sources. The quest for inexpensive food to feed starving people may result in the use of harmful fishing techniques, careless handling of traps, and thoughtless disposal of nets and lines over the reef. Collection of souvenirs, coral, and live aquarium specimens and the removal of coral rock for building material may leave the bottom devoid of life. Frequently, increased tourism means damage caused by boat groundings, improper anchoring and maneuvering, poor diving techniques, and increased nutrient input from tourists' wastes.

Indirect stress results from increased turbidity and siltation caused by coastal development, dredging and filling, channelization, offshore drilling, and increased boating activity. This is further compounded by nutrient enrichment and eutrophication induced by mosquito abatement programs, landscaping and agricultural pollution, offshore disposal, improper sewage treatment, and inadequate septic systems.

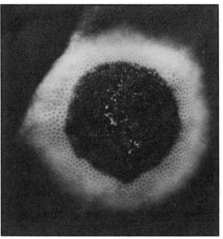

Diseased Jamaican coral.

IMPACT ON THE REEF: WHO IS TO BLAME?

Reef scientists today are developing a clearer understanding of the environmental effects of coastal development, human pollution, and other human-induced disasters. It is not by chance that the healthiest coral reefs are those farthest removed from human activity. Nevertheless, human impact knows no boundaries. Our wastes can be found choking the life from even the most remote tropical reefs.

Each individual land developer, forester, boater, lobsterman, and sport diver perceives his or her own small impact on the coral reef as insignificant. And, if that one impact were the only one, it might in fact be insignificant. The harsh reality is that around the world, millions of people are abusing coral reefs every day. It is not the individual act that is so devastating but the sum of all the millions of acts of carelessness, ignorance, and greed that are destroying the reefs.

Those individuals with proprietary interests in the coral reef would have us believe that the impact of humans is nothing compared with that of nature. However, when human impact is added to the stresses of nature, the changes become too long term and too abrupt for reef organisms to survive.

The ocean environments, especially coral reefs, exist in a fragile balance with the forces of nature that can be easily disrupted. It is absolutely pivotal that we understand the impact of human activity, conscious or unconscious, if coral reefs are to be preserved for future generations.

CHOICES

Our options are limited. There is no easy solution. We must balance human needs and interests with environmental preservation and develop a realistic management plan.

The easy way out would be to allow unlimited human exploitation of the reef and coastal zone without concern for the environment. However, should we make this choice, we have decided that the reefs are not worth saving; that they have no value for coastal protection, food, tourism, or as a unique biological community.

The value of the reefs cannot be expressed merely in dollars and cents; coral reefs are numbered among the natural wonders of the world! They are one of the most biologically diverse ecosystems on this planet, supporting as many as 400 distinct species of coral and over 1,500 different species of fish on a single reef. Nothing on land can surpass the splendor of living coral reefs. We cannot afford their loss.

We could choose to continue as we have been, with limited intervention. However, this option is not working and is having essentially the same impact as doing nothing.

The most difficult decision would be to eliminate all people pressure to reduce pollution and other human impact. This would be the best option for the reef, but because of economics and public opinion, it is not a realistic option.

The best option is to find a balance that allows sensible human contact with the reef without seriously degrading the reef. The realization of this ideal balance has been elusive, but it is not beyond our grasp. The beauty and accessibility of the United States National Park System have demonstrated that we can live in harmony with our environment.

MANAGEMENT AND PRESERVATION TECHNIQUES

The world is beginning to realize that coral reefs are priceless treasures of biologic beauty and richness right-fully belonging to all peoples of the world. As such, they deserve to be protected from unregulated development and uncontrolled exploitation. There is no longer any question of human pressure; its awesome impact is clear and present.

Spotted eagle rays, Jamaica.

Ocean explorer and naturalist William Beebe admonished us to protect our ecosystems when he said, "When the last individual of a race of living things breathes no more, another heaven and another earth must pass before such a one can be again." Throughout the world, marine parks are being set aside by federal law to protect pristine reef ecosystems from rampant development, seabed mining, and hydrocarbon exploration. We don't need to justify the existence of coral reef marine sanctuaries. To the same extent, we need not defend the Grand Canyon's right to exist, neither should we be forced to justify the protection of the living coral reef from those who would exploit it for personal gain.

To understand why current management and preservation techniques are not achieving their purpose, we must examine the steps that have been taken.

Set Aside and Protected

Marine parks and sanctuaries have been set aside by federal and local governments for the enjoyment and benefit of all people. Visitors are treated to the coral reef "experience." They may snorkel in suspended fascination, or scuba dive among spectacular coral formations and visit with hundreds of species of reef fish. The less adventurous can view reef life from the comfort of glass-bottom boats. To a large extent, protection of the reef is up to individual visitors. Each boater, fisherman, snorkeler, and scuba diver has a personal stake in the survival of coral reefs.

For these parks to be effective, interpretive programs must educate, sensitize, and increase visitor awareness of the coral reef ecosystem. People who learn to appreciate the oceanic environment become part of the solution.

Unfortunately, although such protected areas are steadily growing in number and size, they are still relatively limited in worldwide distribution. Some of the best examples are sanctuaries in the United States and Australia.

United States Protected Areas

The United States became involved in reef protection relatively early compared to other countries. Because of marked deterioration of the reefs off Key Largo, in 1960, the State of Florida established the John Pennekamp Coral Reef State Park to protect and preserve from human abuse and predation the only living coral reef in the continental United States. In the days before the park was established, commercial collectors were harvesting corals faster than the corals could regrow. As recently as 1973, visitors were permitted to collect as much as 5 pounds of dead coral per person!

The park quickly became a magnet for fishermen, sport divers, and other reef visitors, stressing the reef ecosystem substantially. In spite of problems caused by increased visitation, the reefs inside the park appeared to fare far better than those outside the protection of the park.

Unfortunately, the state jurisdiction technically ended 3 miles offshore, initially leaving many reefs unprotected. However, by agreement with the federal government, protection was extended to the 300-foot depth. With the contiguous Key Largo National Marine Sanctuary, established in 1975, the protected areas contained coral reefs, seagrass beds, and mangrove swamps covering an area of nearly 180 square miles. Federal protection has gradually been extended, first to Looe Key National Marine Sanctuary and to Biscayne National Park, and finally, in 1990, to all reefs along the coast of the Florida Keys making the Florida Keys National Marine Sanctuary the largest of its kind in the United States.

Australia and the Great Barrier Reef Marine Park

Following the protection plans developed in Florida, Australia recognized the need for management, and in 1980, the Australian government created the Great Barrier Reef Marine Park. The park covers a mosaic of coral reefs and barrier islands and encompasses waters covering nearly 4,700 square miles.

It has been said conservatively that the number of visitors to the Great Barrier Reef during the entire year of 1949, is equalled now in a single day. With the development of enormous, high-speed catamarans, the once remote outer reefs of Australia have become accessible to thousands of tourists every day. Floating hotels permanently anchored over the reefs intensify the human impact.

The establishment of the Great Barrier Reef Marine Park marked a change in management strategy. Instead of merely protecting natural resources by limiting activity, the coral reef environment has been carefully arranged in a series of zones open to a variety of uses. These zones vary from *general use-maximum disturbance* (prohibiting only gas and oil drilling, submarine mining, and spearfishing), to *restricted areas* where only scientific research is allowed. Every possible measure is taken to insure protection of the reef, consistent with maximizing its use. However, despite the Australian government's most carefully planned management strategy, conflicts between mankind and nature continue to occur.

The key phrase is "protection." Typically, anything that threatens the living coral reef is illegal within the park boundaries. A blanket policy, for example, prohibits the breaking, cutting, or displacement of any bottom formation or growth. The removal or destruction of any natural feature or marine life is dealt with harshly as is the dumping of pollutants, refuse, or toxic wastes of any kind. Channelization, dredging and filling, excavating, and construction are also prohibited activities. Under federal law, anyone who does not comply with these regulations is subject to civil penalties of up to A$50,000. Unfortunately, as the number of visitors increases, human impact is inevitable.

Other Marine Parks

In the ensuing years marine parks and underwater sanctuaries have been established in countries around the world. Given financial and technical assistance, many other developing countries would establish similar preserves. Unfortunately, although these parks and sanctuaries have had a positive effect on some reef areas, overall their impact at present is small, as coral reefs around the world continue to be degraded. For example, it is generally agreed that little more than 5 percent of the coral reefs of

Southeast Asia and the eastern Indian Ocean is now in good condition.

Soft coral polyps, Maldives.

Marine parks and sanctuaries do a good job of limiting commercial abuse and uncontrolled exploitation of coral reefs. Much more work needs to be done, however, both inside and outside the sanctuaries. Nowhere in the world are reefs in better condition now than they were before human impact. Additional measures must be taken to help reduce stress and protect coral reefs from neglect and exploitation. In some cases, artificial reefs and alternative dive sites have been established.

Artificial Reefs and Alternative Sites

Some precious underwater gardens grow not on natural substrates, but on structures placed on the sea floor by humans. The major advantage of ship reefs (ships that have rested on the bottom long enough to accumulate a great diversity of hard and soft corals) and other artificial reefs is that they attract fish, lobster, and other mobile organisms. Many shipwrecks around the world, such as those of Truk Lagoon, are renowned for the unique reef systems they've developed, while reducing diver pressure on natural reefs.

At one time artificial reefs were popular and were constructed of a variety of materials, including rubber tires, trucks and automobiles, concrete blocks and pipes, sunken ships, and offshore drilling platforms. However, many of these materials, like rubber tires, are unsuitable for coral growth, and reefs that have grown on steel hulls of ships or car bodies in many instances have deteriorated and fallen apart under the weight of encrustation. Artificial reefs should be constructed of materials, like concrete, that resist corrosion and whose composition is as close as possible to that of a natural reef.

When suitable materials are used, the substrate will be stabilized by algae, bacteria and fire corals, followed by diverse growth of finger corals, clams, oysters, sponges, and purple hydrozoans. The major factor limiting growth appears to be the cumulative effect of deterioration of the artificial-reef substrate and excessive weight of the encrustation, which can cause the structure to collapse.

The most effective use of the artificial reef is in areas where space is a limiting factor for marine organism growth or where it is necessary to reduce diver stress at popular dive sites. In these areas artificial reefs provide protection or a solid substrate on sea bottoms that might not otherwise be habitable. Thus, the artificial reef stimulates an increase in the number of organisms that can live in the area. Unfortunately, most of our past preservational techniques have had limited benefits because they treat the coral reef as a community isolated from surrounding land and coastal environments.

WHAT ELSE MUST BE DONE?

It is easy to be in favor of coral reef preservation, but the steps toward rehabilitation and restoration of the coral reef may be extremely painful. Limits must be imposed on coastal development to preserve swamps and grass beds, and to restrict sedimentation and nutrient input near shore. New ways must be found to dispose of wastes. People must be made aware of the impact of nutrients and various chemicals on the world's coral reefs. Sound management principles are necessary if we are to limit the physical and chemical damage caused by tourism, boating, collecting, and diving.

Beyond the obvious, we must embark on a determined program of coral reef restoration. If people are ready to support a pollution-free sea and a clean environment for healthy coral reefs, they must be prepared to boycott the purveyors of aquarium fish, reef corals, and coral jewelry.

We face a crisis that endangers coral reef communities because we have allowed inadequate environmental safeguards to be adopted. The time has come to express public concern and support legislation that will help to clean up our environment.

Legislation

There is no longer any question of the need for legislation to protect the unique, irreplaceable coral reefs, but legislation without education and enforcement is meaningless. Laws must be enacted to require evidence that coastal development will not adversely impact mangrove swamps, seagrass meadows, or the coral reef itself. Violators must be prosecuted and penalized to the full extent of the law, and fines should be heavy enough to discourage would-be violators.

Cities must be prevented from dumping human wastes into the sea. Many reefs north of Key West are loaded with the blue-green bacteria that cause the lethal black-band disease. The dominance of the filamentous algae and bacteria may be linked to the daily discharge of 8 million gallons of Key West's nutrient-enriched sewage into the ocean.

All over the world human wastes leach into sea water and carry high levels of phosphates and nitrates into the reef environment. However, the technology exists to build safe sanitary systems that would have an immediate positive effect on the corals and the ocean waters. Regrettably, legislators are not excited about enacting unpopular legislation, no matter how important or expensive.

Zoning

Every coral reef in the world has the potential to produce millions of dollars in revenue. Studies are now under way to develop reef management plans that would provide a working relationship between the social, cultural, ecological, and economic needs of the coral reef and its managing country.

It is well past time that we admit that the coral reefs are being killed by industry and by people. Having taken that step, we can begin to define the action necessary to reverse the devastating human impact on the coral reef ecosystem. Now is the time to develop and deploy a resource and environmental management and protection plan.

More effective and more closely scrutinized zoning regulations must be developed. Perhaps the same mechanism could monitor the discharge and runoff of troublesome industrial and agricultural wastes.

Such tactics may be unpopular, but they will be necessary. Other reefs should be subjected to limited public access. Very few reefs should be open to unrestricted activity.

Research - Baseline Studies

There is reason to suspect that we are courting catastrophic coral diseases that can affect the vitality of coral reefs around the world. The frequency of mass mortalities affecting reef organisms appears to be increasing with each decade. Bleaching events, band diseases, and mass mortalities, such as that of long-spined sea urchins in the Caribbean, have marked the 1980s.

If we are to prevent the die-off associated with such events, we must find the money to fund research to investigate the causes of disease. Once the causes are identified, the steps necessary to prevent mass mortalities must be taken, but, the progress of such research is slow and its full impact may not be obvious for years. Can we afford to wait for 25 years to discover what our greed has wrought?

The impact of decades of human activity on coral reefs is uncertain. One thing is clear: only by continuous long-term monitoring of the effects of various stresses on the coral reef community can the reefs be saved. Those human activities that threaten the survival of coral reefs must be halted if we are to prevent further deterioration of reefs around the world.

We need to embark on a program of research that will help us understand the nature and extent of present impact. Armed with that knowledge, we will be able to answer such questions as "how many people are too many?"

Public Awareness

Only by increasing public awareness can long-term protection of coral reefs and associated environments be achieved. Preservation of coral reefs will be possible only when each person who is in direct or indirect contact with the reef is made aware of the problems he or she poses to the coral reef ecosystem.

It has been said that no one doubts the value of coral reefs, but *value* is a subjective word. To the oil industry, it is cash on the barrelhead. To an impoverished fisherman in a developing country, it is food for his children. In affluent nations, it is the aesthetics of the reefs and the preservation of the richest of diverse communities.

Is it possible to educate people in developing countries to understand the potential of the reef, the aesthetic value, the economic significance of the reef to the host country? The answer is a qualified yes. In the Philippines and Jamaica, for example, educational programs for fishermen, sponsored by marine laboratories and marine parks, have made promising strides.

Typically, the fishermen are more interested in economic return than in environmental impact. Even so, as fishermen are included in the decision-making process, planning, and program implementation, the results are significant. Offered nondestructive alternatives with the potential for reasonable economic reward, the local fishermen are cooperative.

The coral reef can be saved with knowledge provided to each individual. The imperative for action demands unqualified support, lots of hard work, and determination. The coral reef's survival demands knowledge and understanding.

Education

It has been suggested by more than one environmentalist that many septic systems in use in the Florida Keys do not conform to existing Florida sanitary codes. How do you tell retirees in the Florida Keys that their toilets are threatening one of the most important reef systems in the world with extinction? The answer can only be found through education. No right-thinking citizen wants the reef to die, but it's understandably difficult for a senior citizen to see the cause-and-effect trail leading back to him or her. A way must be found to make people understand. It is well past time that citizens and elected law-makers alike understand not only the ecologic, biologic, and economic value of the coral reef, but also, as importantly, the many ways the reef is being destroyed by humans.

Before we can preserve and protect the coral reefs, we must learn how to limit human impact on them. Globally, the prognosis is not favorable. At the tip of the Sinai peninsula are some of the most extraordinary reefs in the world. Because of the explosive development of tourism in this area of Egypt, unregulated development and equally unregulated recreational use of the reefs have caused substantial reef degradation in less than one year. The same is true in third-world countries everywhere.

More than 30 percent of the world's coral reefs is in Southeast Asia and eastern Indian Ocean waters. These reefs historically have had the greatest diversity and abundance of living cor-

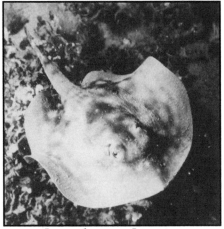

Juvenile ray, Jamaica.

als in the world. Now, they may be undergoing a negative dynamic change faster than any other coral reefs in the world. Currently more than 70 percent of the reefs in those areas is significantly degraded.

There are ways to enjoy the gifts of the reef with minimum impact. Sharing those best-kept secrets is a sound plan whose time has come.

HERE FOR THE NEXT GENERATION?

Only time will determine whether coral reefs will become algal reefs. There is no question as to the impact of human activities on the vitality of the coral reef ecosystem. The reefs of the world are seriously threatened *now*.

It is a testament to the inherent durability of the reef ecosystem that it has managed to survive the last hundred years of human impact. Despite the combined great forces of destruction: deforestation, dynamite fishing, waste disposal, outbreaks of *Acanthaster planci*, epidemics of disease, hurricanes and violent waves, typhoon rains and freshwater runoff, dredging and sedimentation, coral mining, and high-intensity farming; the coral reefs have survived! However, their survival may only be a matter of time.

There is an obvious degradation in the quality of reef waters surrounding the reefs of Florida. Many people reading this have seen the transition from the absolute transparency of the early 1940s to the heavily silted waters we see today. The oceans dominate our Earth. The same ocean water that touches the Florida reefs touches a reef in Australia on the other side of the planet. We are all children of the sea, and we must act now if we are to act at all. There can be no more waiting until we have a perfect solution. To continue our present environmental course holds only disaster.

Perhaps the coral seas can inspire us to live in communion with nature. Is it possible that we humans can turn away from our present course of destruction to a life of harmony? Can we understand that the individual can make a difference?

There's a story about a child throwing starfish back into the sea after an unusually violent storm had thrown them up high above the receding tide. A man watched bemused as the boy hurried to each dying starfish and threw it as far out into the sea as he could. "You're wasting your time, kid," said the man pointing down the beach to where thousands of starfish lay dying. "It won't matter." The child picked up another, and throwing it into the sea, he replied, " . . . it does to this one."

"Reverence for all life must be
at the center of man's bahavior."
— Albert Schweitzer

GLOSSARY

ADAPTATION: adjustment of an organism to its environment through the process of natural selection

ADDUCTOR MUSCLE: muscle that holds the shells of a bivalved mollusk or brachiopod together

AHERMATYPIC: not reef forming, commonly referring to small, solitary scleractinian corals that do not build reefs

ALCYONARIAN CORAL: soft coral with a skeleton composed of protein material and calcareous spicules, includes whip corals

ALGAE (sing. ALGA): marine or freshwater simple plant forms that lack true leaves, stems, or roots; nonvascular, plants lacking conductive or supportive tissues

ALKALINE: basic (rather than acid) liquid with a pH greater than 7.0

ALTERNATION OF GENERATIONS: orderly succession of sexual and asexual reproduction in the life cycle of such animals as foraminifera or cnidarians

AMOEBOID CELL: single cell with an irregular shape that moves by cytoplasmic pressure differences or pseudopodia

AMPHINEURA: see polyplacophora

AMPHIPOD: elongate, laterally compressed crustacean, includes the sand hopper

ANEMONE: solitary cnidarian polyp lacking a hard skeleton

ANNELID: segmented worm

ANNULARIS ZONE: the forereef escarpment of Caribbean reefs, typified by growth of *Montastrea annularis*

ANTHOZOAN: cnidarian whose life cycle consists of only polyps with no medusa stage

ANTIPATHARIAN: colonial corals with a horny axial skeleton, includes the black corals

ARAGONITE: see calcium carbonate

ARISTOTLE'S LANTERN: calcareous chewing structure or "jaw" in the echinoids

ARTHROPOD: segmented animal with jointed appendages and a hard exterior covering

ASCIDIAN: tunicate or sea squirt, colonial or solitary chordate with a sack-like body

ASEXUAL: reproduction by dividing or budding, not involving the union of eggs and sperm

ASTEROID: star fish

ATOLL: ring-like or oval coral reef with a central lagoon

ATOLLON: a large atoll that consists of many smaller atolls

BACK REEF: area between the reef crest and land; shallow area behind the reef or away from the open ocean

BAFFLE: something that deflects or decreases the velocity of water

BAND DISEASE: infection of corals caused by cyanobacteria that may lead to the death of the coral

BANK: a large area that rises above the sea floor, a submerged plateau

BANK REEF: a reef rising from the continental shelf and covering a large area, generally irregular in shape, surrounded by deep water

BARREN ZONE: in Caribbean reefs, the region seaward of the lower *palmata* zone and landward of the buttress or mixed zone

BARRIER REEF: a reef separated from adjacent land by a lagoon

BENTHOS: organism living on or in the bottom or sea floor

BILATERAL SYMMETRY: having right and left sides that are mirror images

BIOLUMINESCENCE: production of light by living organisms due to complex internal chemical reactions

BIVALVE: mollusk having two shells, includes clams, oysters, scallops, and mussels

BRACHIOPOD: lamp shell, an animal with two shells like the bivalved mollusks, but with a lophophore for feeding, no foot, and having bilaterally symmetrical shells

BREAKER ZONE: region where waves break

BROOD: incubation of eggs

BRYOZOAN: moss animal, colonial, small animals with a lophophore

BUTTRESS ZONE: region of the reef dominated by huge boulder corals forming ridges or elongate mounds seaward of the *palmata* zone in Caribbean reefs

CALCAREA: class of sponges having calcareous spicules

CALCAREOUS: formed of lime or calcium carbonate

CALCITE: see calcium carbonate

CALCIUM CARBONATE: mineral made of calcium and carbonate (commonly calcite or aragonite), a common shell material

CARAPACE: chitonous or calcareous external covering of the cephalothorax of crustacean arthropods

CEPHALOPOD: mollusks that have tentacles surrounding the mouth, commonly having a reduced internal shell or no shell, includes the octopus, cuttlefish, and squid

CEPHALOTHORAX: fused head and midsection (thorax) of some arthropods

CERVICORNIS ZONE: corresponds to the forereef terrace of Caribbean reefs, typified by growth of *Acropora cervicornis*

CHEMOSYNTHESIS: process by which food and energy may be produced by chemical reactions in such organisms as bacteria

CHITON: see polyplacophora

CHOANOCYTE: a flagellated collar cell found lining the interior of a sponge, responsible for feeding, respiration, and generating water currents

CHORDATE: an animal having a notochord and dorsal nerve chord, includes tunicates and vertebrates

CHROMATOPHORE: colored pigment

CILIA (sing. CILIUM): minute, hair-like structures usually associated with feeding, locomotion, or respiration

CIRRI (sing. CIRRUS): slender arm or appendage

CIRRIPEDIA: subclass of crustaceans with six pairs of appendages that strain food from water and having an external calcareous housing, includes the barnacles

CLIMAX COMMUNITY: terminal association of organisms in a succession of associations, in equilibrium with the environment

CLONE: an individual or group of individuals descended asexually from a single parent

CNIDARIAN: a radially symmetrical organism having one opening into a digestive cavity, possessing two tissue layers, cnidoblasts, and having polyp and/or medusa body forms, includes corals, anemones, jellyfish, and hydrozoans

CNIDOBLAST: stinging cell possessed by a cnidarian, contains a nematocyst used in defense or capture of prey

CNIDOCIL: filament or thread on the tip of a cnidoblast that releases the nematocyst

COELENTERATE: old term applied primarily to cnidarians, but originally included comb jellies and sponges

COMB JELLY: a member of the Phylum Ctenophora, gelatinous, more or less spherical organism having 8 rows of ciliated "combs" for locomotion and 2 tentacles to capture prey, most lack nematocysts

COMMENSALISM: relationship between two organisms in which one organism benefits and the other is neither benefited nor harmed

COMMUNITY: organisms that inhabit and interact within a definable area or region

CONSUMER: an organism that does not produce its own food

CONTINENTAL SHELF: flat or gently sloping margin of a continental mass

CONVECTION CURRENTS: movement of a liquid (or gas) caused by a difference in density

COPEPOD: microscopic crustacean with a rounded body and oar-like swimming appendages, most are planktonic and are an important part of the ocean food chain

CORAL: benthic cnidarians that possess a skeleton

CRINOID: sea lilies, including the stalked echinoderms

CRUSTACEAN: arthropods with a calcareous exoskeleton and antennae, includes the lobsters, crabs, shrimp, barnacles and copepods

CTENOPHORE: comb jelly

CUBOMEDUSA: small jellyfish with 4 sides and 4 tentacles or groups of tentacles bearing nematocysts, body is higher than wide

CYANOBACTERIA: blue-green, photosynthetic prokaryotes (single-celled organisms lacking a well-defined nucleus)

CYTOPLASM: cell fluid lying outside the nucleus

DACTYLOPORES: small holes in hydrozoan skeleton in which dactylozooids live

DACTYLOZOOIDS: specialized tactile polyps in the hydrozoans

DECAPOD: crustaceans having 5 pairs of walking legs, includes the crabs, shrimp, and lobsters

DEEP SEA DRILLING PROJECT: ocean bottom sampling program sponsored by the U.S. government and others

DEMOSPONGIA: sponges whose skeleton is primarily formed of spongin, an organic fibrous network; silica spicules may also be present

DEPOSIT/DETRITUS FEEDER: any organism that ingests organic particulate matter or sediment mixed with organic matter from on top of or within the sea floor

DERMAL PORES: openings that take water into a sponge

DINOFLAGELLATE: microscopic "flame" alga

DIVERSITY: the number of different species of organisms present in an area

DORSAL: back or upper surface

DUGONG: Indo-Pacific aquatic, herbivorous mammal related to the manatee or sea cow, possessing a bilobate tail like that of a whale

ECHINODERM: spiny-skinned animals with an articulated, calcareous internal skeleton, 5-fold radial or biradial symmetry, and a water vascular system, includes crinoids, sea urchins, star fish, brittle stars, and sea cucumbers

ECHINOID: globular or flattened echinoderms including sea urchins, sand dollars, and sea biscuits

ECOSYSTEM: interrelationship of all the biological and physical environmental factors in a community

ECTOPARASITE: parasites living on the outer surface of an organism

EL NINO - SOUTHERN OSCILLATION: southerly flowing warm current off the west coast of South America that develops due to an abnormal high-pressure system in the western Pacific

EMERSION: exposure above water

ENDEMIC: related to or native to a specific region

EPIDERMIS: outer cell layer

EROSION: weathering and removal of sediment on the Earth's crust

ERRANT: not living within tubes or burrows

EUTROPHICATION: condition of abundant to excessive nutrients and organic matter in an environment

EVISCERATE: to remove or eject internal body organs

EXOSKELETON: external skeleton or covering

FARO: small atoll-shaped or oblong reef with a lagoon that may be as deep as 30 meters, formed on the rim of a barrier reef or lagoon

FILTER FEEDER: organism that obtains food by straining small organic particles from the water

FLAGELLA (sing. FLAGELLUM): whip-like structures used for locomotion or water-current movement and feeding by some organisms including protozoans and sponges

FORAMINIFERA: small single-celled animals having a test or shell commonly formed of calcium carbonate

FOREREEF: region seaward of the reef crest

FOREREEF ESCARPMENT: abrupt slope or cliff below the forereef terrace of Caribbean reefs

FOREREEF SLOPE: a sand-covered incline below the forereef escarpment of Caribbean reefs

FOREREEF TERRACE: relatively flat upper part of the forereef of Caribbean reefs, extending seaward from the base of the buttress or mixed zone

FRINGING REEF: reef lying adjacent to land with no backreef lagoon

FUNNEL: fleshy anterior tube-like extension of the mantle in cephalopods

GASTRODERMIS: inner cell layer that lines body organs

GASTROPOD: mollusks possessing a body that has undergone torsion commonly with an undivided, spiral shell, includes the snails, slugs, and nudibranchs

GASTROPORES: larger holes in hydrozoan skeleton in which gastrozooids live

GASTROVASCULAR CAVITY: digestive cavity or stomach

GASTROZOOIDS: polyps specialized for digestion in the hydrozoans

GLACIAL-ACTIVITY THEORY: theory first proposed by Daly that rising sea level following the Ice Age was responsible for forming, in order, fringing reefs, barrier reefs, and atolls

GLACIER: mass of ice with definite boundaries, formed by recrystallization of snow, flowing slowly over the land's surface

GORGONIAN: soft coral with a horny central axis and calcareous spicules, includes sea fans, sea feathers, and plumes

GORGONIN: hard organic material forming the horny skeleton of the soft corals

GREENHOUSE EFFECT: warming of the Earth's climate due to the trapping of heat near the Earth's surface because of the atmospheric buildup of carbon dioxide

HARD GROUND: a sediment-free, rock surface exposed on the sea floor commonly in shallow, lagoonal environments

HERMAPHRODITIC: possessing both male and female reproductive organs

HERMATYPIC: reef forming, commonly referring to corals that have photosynthetic zooxanthellae living in their tissues

HEXACTINELLIDAE: glass sponges, class of sponges that have a skeleton formed of triaxon siliceous spicules

HOLOTHURIAN: sea cucumber

HYDROZOAN: polypoid cnidarian with a reduced medusa stage, includes fire corals, Portuguese man of war, and lace corals

HYPERSALINE: above normal salinity

ICE AGE: an interval of continental glaciation

INSHORE ZONE: interface between land and the reef

INVERTEBRATES: animals lacking a backbone, the so-called "lower" animals

ISLAND SLOPE: hard, rocky substrate below the deep forereef of Caribbean reefs at depths of 120 to 300 meters

ISOPOD: dorso-ventrally flattened crustaceans, many of which are scavengers or parasites on other crustaceans or fish

KNOLL: small mounds of limited extent rising less than 1,000 meters from the ocean floor

LAGOON: a partially or completely restricted coastal bay that has less freshwater influx than an estuary

LAGOONAL ZONE: area occupied by a backreef lagoon

LARVA (pl. LARVAE): an immature animal whose form differs from the adult stage

LEEWARD: toward land, sheltered from the wind

LIMESTONE: a rock composed primarily of calcium carbonate (lime)

LOPHOPHORE: ciliated feeding structure of animals such as the brachiopods, bryozoans, and phoronid worms

LOWER *PALMATA* ZONE: part of the reef crest seaward of the main *palmata* zone of Caribbean reefs

MAGNETITE: black-mineral form of iron oxide with magnetic properties, secreted as radula teeth by some mollusks

MANATEE: sea cow, a large, herbivorous, aquatic mammal

MANGROVE: tropical tree or shrub with prop roots, growing in shallow water along low-lying coasts

MANTLE: extension of the soft tissue of mollusks and brachiopods responsible for secreting the shell

MASS EXTINCTION: the dying out of many groups of organisms on a global scale during a brief interval of geologic time

MEDUSA: the free-swimming stage or body form of a cnidarian in which the mouth and surrounding tentacles face downward, a jelly fish

MESENTERIAL FILAMENTS: thread-like extensions produced from the free margins of polyp mesenteries, having nematocysts and digestive enzymes

MESENTERIAL TISSUE: radially arranged fleshy tissue dividing the inside of the gastrovascular cavity of a polyp

MESENTERIES: vertical, radially arranged partitions lining the inside of the gastrovascular cavity of a polyp, lying adjacent to the septa in scleractinian corals

MESOGLEA: amorphous, jellylike, cellular material between the inner and outer tissue layers of cnidarians

MICRO-ATOLL: a ring-shaped colony or circular growth of a coral head or serpulid worm colony, commonly 1 to 6 meters across, that develops in intertidal regions

MIXED ZONE: diverse zone of coral growth below the lower *palmata* zone of Caribbean reefs

MOLLUSKS: invertebrates with an unsegmented body, commonly protected by a calcareous shell, includes bivalves, chitons, gastropods, cephalopods, and others

MORPHOLOGY: shape

MUTUALISM: symbiotic relationship in which both organisms benefit

NEKTON: swimming organisms that control their movement through the water

NEMATOCYST: stinging mechanism within a cnidoblast, either sticky or containing poison for entrapping prey

NEMERTEA: ribbon worm

NOTOCHORD: flexible longitudinal rod lying between the digestive tract and nerve system in chordates

NUDIBRANCH: snail that has no protective shell as an adult

NUTRIENTS: organic or inorganic compounds used by plants for photosynthesis, important examples are nitrogen and phosphorous compounds

OOZE: fine sediment that contains at least 30 percent biogenic skeletal material

OPERCULUM: top shell or cap covering an aperture

OPHIUROID: brittle star

OPPORTUNIST: organism with a high reproductive rate when the environment is favorable

OSCULUM: large, often elevated, opening through which water is flushed from a sponge

OUTER SLOPE: deep forereef zone of Indo-Pacific reefs, corresponds to forereef zones below the forereef terrace of Caribbean reefs

PALMATA ZONE: region of dense growth of *Acropora palmata* in Caribbean reefs, corresponds to the breaker zone

PEDICLE: muscular stalk or support by which a brachiopod may attach to the sea floor

PELAGIC: open ocean

PERTURBATION: an abnormal stress or abnormal event in a living community

PH: acidity or alkalinity of a liquid

PHORONID: tube worms with a horseshoe-shaped lophophore

PHOTOSYNTHESIS: process by which plants convert carbon dioxide and water to simple carbohydrates in the presence of light

PHYTOPLANKTON: floating photosynthetic organisms

PINACOCYTE: outer, protective cell of a sponge

PINNACLE REEF: a reef shaped like a spire or pillar with a pointed top

PINNATE: feathered or leaf-like projections or appendages on either side of a central axis

PINNULES: feather-like lateral appendages, such as those on crinoid arms

PLANKTIVOROUS: organism that eats plankton

PLANKTON: floating or weakly swimming organisms that cannot control their movement through the water

PLANULA: larval stage of a cnidarian

PLATE: a segment of the Earth's crust that moves independently of the other layers of the Earth

PLATE TECTONICS THEORY: explanation of the mechanism by which large parts of the Earth's surface are formed, moved, or destroyed

PLATFORM REEF: shallow reef built on a level-to-gently sloping surface

PLATYHELMENTHES: flat worm

PLEISTOCENE EPOCH: time of last glacial advances in North America, earlier part of the Quaternary Period

POLYCHAETE WORM: marine, segmented worm

POLYP: sessile stage or life form of a cnidarian, a cylindrical sack or tube-shaped animal with tentacles surrounding the mouth that lies on the upper surface

POLYPLACOPHORA: molluscan class that includes the chitons, which possess a shell composed of eight calcareous plates

PORIFERA: sponge

PRIMARY PRODUCER: organism that makes its own food, an autotroph

PROBOSCIS: tubular protrusion or elongation of the head or snout

PRODUCTIVITY: amount of organic matter synthesized by an organism from inorganic sources

PROTOZOAN: single-celled animals with a well-defined cell nucleus

RADIAL SYMMETRY: repetition of parts around a center

RADULA: file-like "tongue" or rasping structure of many mollusks

REAR ZONE: region on the lagoon side of the reef crest

REEF: a wave resistant, organic structure

REEF CREST: shallowest region of the reef, includes the rear zone, reef flat, and rubble zone

REEF FLAT: platform of coral fragments and sand that is exposed at low tide

REEF FRONT: upper seaward face of Indo-Pacific reefs, corresponds to forereef zones above the forereef escarpment of Caribbean reefs

REEF ROCK: limestone formed by the cementing together of reef organisms

REGENERATE: ability to regrow lost body parts

RIBBON REEF: an exceptionally long, narrow reef with curved ends formed along the edge of the continental shelf

RUBBLE ZONE: shallowest part of the reef crest that consists of broken coral fragments

SABELLID WORM: segmented tube worm with a shell composed of shell fragments or organic material, includes feather duster worms

SALINITY: dissolved salt content of a liquid expressed in parts per thousand

SCLERACTINIAN: corals with a calcareous skeleton

SCLERODERMITE: bundle of calcareous needles forming the skeleton of scleractinian corals

SCLEROSPONGES: sponges with a massive calcareous skeleton and siliceous spicules

SCYPHOZOAN: true jellyfish, medusa form is dominant and polyp body form is reduced or absent

SEAFLOOR SPREADING: process by which new sea floor (oceanic crust) is formed at oceanic ridges and pushed outward toward trenches by younger crust

SEAWARD SLOPE: Caribbean reef zones extending from the forereef terrace to the forereef slope

SECCHI DISK: device for measuring water transparency or clarity

SEDENTARY: immobile, tube- or burrow-dwelling animal

SEDIMENT: solid material that has been transported and deposited on the Earth's surface

SEDIMENTATION: accumulation of sediment deposited by water, air, ice or gravity

SEPTAE (sing. SEPTUM): a vertical partition of the skeleton of an organism, such as a coral

SERPULID WORM: calcareous or leathery tube worm that lives within the substrate

SESSILE: fixed, immobile, or attached to the bottom

SETAE (sing. SETA): hair-like projections on the exoskeleton or covering of arthropods and annelids

SIPHUNCLE: fleshy posterior extension of the mantle in cephalopods

SPICULE: mineralized skeletal element of a sponge or gorgonian

SPONGIN: organic-fiber network that forms the skeleton of demosponges

SPUR-AND-GROOVE SYSTEM: alternating sand channels and coral-covered mounds extending seaward from the reef crest

STOMATOPODA: mantis shrimp

SUBMERGENCE THEORY: theory proposed by Darwin that subsidence of volcanic islands was responsible for forming, in order, fringing reefs, barrier reefs, and atolls

SUBSTRATE: sediment or rock surface of the sea floor, the base or foundation

SURGE CHANNEL: transverse channel cutting across the outer edge of a coral reef, water level fluctuates with wave energy

SYMBIONT: usually the smaller of two partners participating in symbiosis

SYMBIOSIS: intimate association of two organisms of different species, one or both may benefit, includes mutualism, commensalism, and parasitism

TABLE REEF: flat-topped reef that rises from the sea floor

TECTONICS: earth movement or the rock structures that result from such movement

TENTACLES: sensory or food-gathering projections usually surrounding the mouth

TERRIGENOUS: land derived

THORAX: body region between the head and tail

TIDAL POOL: depression that collects water on a tidal flat

TIDAL RANGE: difference between high and low tides

TOPOGRAPHY: configuration of a surface (for example, the sea floor)

TROPICS: region between 30° north or south of the equator

TUBE FEET: echinoderm suction cup-like projections that move by varying water pressure

TUNICATE: globular or cylindrical sack-like animal possessing a notochord and gill slits, may be colonial or solitary, sea squirts

TURBIDITY: amount of suspended solids in a liquid

VAGRANT: mobile

VENTRAL: underside

VERMETID: worm-like

VERTEBRATE: having a backbone

VISCERA: internal body organs

WALL: deepest part of a Caribbean reef, a vertical cliff corresponding to the upper deep forereef

WATER VASCULAR SYSTEM: water canal network in echinoderms that generally terminates in tube feet used for gas exchange, locomotion, food handling, or sensory reception

WINDWARD: direction from which the wind blows

ZOANTHID: colonial polyps without skeletons

ZOANTHUS ZONE: area of the reef flat covered with zoanthids

ZOOID: individual member in a colony of animals, for example, a single bryozoan animal

ZOOPLANKTON: floating non-photosynthesizing organisms

ZOOXANTHELLAE: unicellular, photosynthetic dinoflagellates present as symbionts in hermatypic corals, mollusks, protozoans, and other organisms

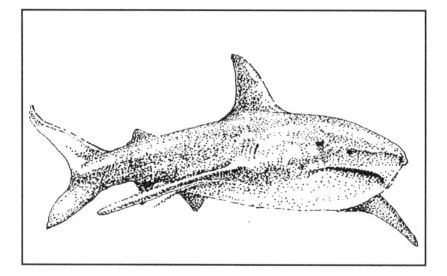

Bull shark.

BIBLIOGRAPHY

Atwood, D. K., J. Burton, J. E. Corredor, G. R. Harrey, A. J. Mata-Jimenez, A. Vasquez-Botello, and B. A. Wade, 1987, Petroleum production in the Caribbean: Oceanus, v. 30, no. 4, p. 25-32.

Barnes, D. J., B. E. Chalker, D. W. Kinsey, 1986, Reef metabolism: Oceanus, v. 29, no. 2, p. 20-26.

Birkland, Charles, 1989, The Faustian traits of the crown-of-thorns starfish: American Scientist, v. 77, p. 154-162.

Bondareff, J. M., 1988, The M/V Wellwood grounding - a sanctuary case study - the legal issues: Oceanus, v. 31, no. 1, p. 44-45.

Bright, T. J., W. C. Jaap, and C. Cashman, 1981, Ecology and management of coral reefs and organic banks, in Proceedings of Environmental Research Needs in the Gulf of Mexico: U. S. Department of Commerce, NOAA - ERL, Miami, Florida, p. 53-160.

Chesher, R. H., 1975, Biological impact of a large scale desalination plant at Key West, Florida, in E. J. Ferguson Wood and R. E. Johannes (ed.), Tropical Marine Pollution: Elsevier, New York City, N. Y., p. 99-153.

Colin, P. I., 1978, Caribbean Reef Invertebrates and Plants - A Field Guide to the Invertebrates and Plants Occurring on Coral Reefs of the Caribbean, the Bahamas, and Florida: T. F. H. Publications, Neptune City, N. J., 506 p.

Daly, R. A., 1910, Pleistocene glaciation and the coral reef problem: American Journal of Science, series 4, v. 30, p. 297-308.

Dana, J. D., 1872, Corals and Coral Islands: Dodd and Mead, New York City, N. Y., 398 p.

Darwin, Charles, 1842, The Structure and Distribution of Coral Reefs: Smith, Elder and Co., London, 214 p.

Endean, Robert, 1982, Australia's Great Barrier Reef: University of Queensland Press, St. Lucia, Queensland, Australia, 348 p.

Ginsburg, R. N. and H. Lowenstam, 1958, The influence of marine bottom communities on the depositional environment of sediments: Journal of Geology, v. 66, p. 310-18.

Gittings, S. R. and T. J. Bright, 1988, The M/V Wellwood grounding - a sanctuary case study - the science: Oceanus, v. 31, no. 1, p. 36-41.

Goodwin, Mel, 1987, Changing times for Caribbean fisheries: Oceanus, v. 30, no. 4, p. 55-64.

Goreau, T. F., 1959, The ecology of Jamaican coral reefs I. species composition and zonation: Ecology, v. 40, p. 67-90.

Goreau, T. F. and N. I. Goreau, 1973, The ecology of Jamaican reefs II. geomorphology, zonation, and sedimentary phases: Bulletin of Marine Science, v. 23, p. 399-464.

Goreau, T. F., N. I. Goreau, and T. J. Goreau, 1979, Corals and coral reefs: Scientific American, v. 241, no. 2, p. 124-36.

Harrigan, W. J., 1988, The M/V Wellwood grounding - a sanctuary case study - coping with disaster: Oceanus, v. 31, no. 1, p. 42-43.

Heckel, P. H., 1974, Carbonate buildups in the geologic record, in L. F. Laporte (ed.), Reefs in Time and Space - selected examples from the recent and ancient: Society of Economic Paleontologists and Mineralogists Sp. Publ. 18, p. 90-154.

Holland, Robert, 1985, Coral reef research and the Wellwood Incident: Sea Frontiers, v. 31, no. 1, p. 29-35.

Hopley, David and P. J. Davies, 1986, The evolution of the Great Barrier Reef: Oceanus, v. 29, no. 2, p. 6-12.

Humann, Paul, 1983, Ocean Realm Guide to Corals of Florida, the Bahamas, and the Caribbean: Ocean Realm Publ. Corp., Miami, FL, 80 p.

Jaap, W. C. and J. K. Adams, 1984, The Ecology of South Florida Coral Reefs - A Community Profile: U. S. Fish and Wildlife Service FWS/OBS-82/08, 138 p.

Johannes, R. E., 1975, Pollution and degradation of coral reef communities, *in* E. J. Ferguson-Wood and R. E. Johannes (eds.), Tropical Marine Pollution: Elsevier, New York City, N.Y., p. 13-20.

Kaplan, Eugene, 1982, Field Guide to Coral Reefs of the Caribbean and Florida: Houghton-Mifflin Co., Boston, Mass., 271 p.

Kelleher, Graeme, 1986, Managing the Great Barrier Reef: Oceanus, v. 29, no. 2, p. 13-19.

Kuhlmann, D. H. H., 1985, Living Coral Reefs of the World (Translation of Das lebende Riff): Arco Publishing Inc., New York City, N. Y., 185 p.

Ladd, H. S., 1977, Types of coral reefs and their distribution, *in* O. A. Jones and R. Endean (eds.), Biology and Geology of Coral Reefs, Geology 2, v. 4: Academic Press, New York City, N. Y., p. 1-20.

LaPoint, B. E., 1989, Caribbean coral reefs - are they becoming algal reefs: Sea Frontiers, v. 35, no. 2, p. 83-91.

Levine, J. S. and J. L. Rotman, 1985, Undersea Life: Stewart, Tabori & Chang, New York City, N. Y., 223 p.

Lucas, John, 1986, The Crown of Thorns Starfish: Oceanus, v. 29, no. 2, p. 55-64.

Newell, N. D., 1972, The evolution of reefs: Scientific American, v. 226, no. 6, p. 54-65.

PADI, 1988, The aquatic realm, *in* The Encyclopedia of Recreational Diving: PADI Inc., Santa Ana, Calif., p. 4:1-74.

Shinn, E. A., 1989, What is really killing the corals: Sea Frontiers, v. 35, no. 2, p. 72-81.

Stoddart, D. R., 1969, Ecology and morphology of recent coral reefs: Biological Reviews of the Cambridge Philosophical Society, v. 44, no. 4, p. 433-98.

Suman, D. O., 1987, Intermediate technologies for small-scale fishermen in the Caribbean: Oceanus, v. 30, no. 4, p. 65-68.

Veron, J. E. N., 1986, Distribution of reef-building corals: Oceanus, v. 29, no. 2, p. 27-31.

Voss, G. L., 1988, Coral Reefs of Florida: Pineapple Press, Sarasota, Fl., 69 p.

Wallace, C. C., R. C. Babcock, P. L. Harrison, J. K. Oliver, and B. L. Willis, 1986, Sex on the reef - mass spawning of corals: Oceanus, v. 29, no. 2, p. 38-42.

Wells, J. W., 1957, Coral reefs, in J. Hedgpeth (ed.), Treatise on Marine Ecology and Paleoecology, v. 1 (Ecology): Geological Society of America Memoir 67, p. 609-31.

White, A. T., 1987, Coral Reefs - Valuable Resources of Southeast Asia: International Center for Living Aquatic Resources Management, Education Series 1, Manila, Philippines, 36 p.

Wilkinson, C. R., 1986, The nutritional spectrum of coral reef benthos: Oceanus, v. 29, no. 2, p. 69-75.

Williams, E. H. Jr and L. B. Williams, 1987, Caribbean marine mass mortalities - a problem with a solution: Oceanus, v. 30, no. 4, p. 69-75.

Williams, L. B. and E. H. Williams, Jr., 1988, Coral Reef Bleaching - current crisis, future warning: Sea Frontiers, v. 34, no. 2, p. 80-87.

Wood, E. M., 1983, Reef Corals of the World, Biology and Field Guide: T. F. H. Publications, Neptune City, N. J., 256 p.

INDEX

Bold page numbers indicate illustrations and photographs.

ACKNOWLEDGMENTS

Palaces Under the Sea examines the remarkable diversity of one of the richest biotic communities on the planet. In the preparation of this book, the authors have stood on the shoulders of many of the world's finest coral reef scientists. A number of scientists, academicians, and diving educators reviewed the manuscript and provided critical input which was and is greatly appreciated. Nevertheless, the authors alone bear the responsibility for any materials appearing in this book. The efforts of Dr. O. T. Hayward and Donna M. Corey particularly are acknowledged with gratitude.

In circumnavigating our watery planet, we met and were often supported by governments, organizations, and individuals. Two in particular stand out. They are Ben Concepcion of Saipan and Cdr. Harry Francis USN (ret.). We cannot begin to express our gratitude for their friendship and stewardship of the sea's resources. The support of Kodak Australia is greatly appreciated. The National Aeronautics and Space Administration provided the photograph of the Earth from space, Key Largo National Marine Sanctuary provided the photograph of the Wellwood, Jimmie C. Smith supplied the photograph of the Belize atoll, and Chris Hansen, Baylor University Photography, photographed the authors. The artwork was created by Peggy Grinvalsky, Donna Corey, Rena Bonem, and Denise Macko.

Each of these people is part of the growing eco-conscience of our imperiled planet. They share a vision of our future on a living planet whose bounty will continue to blossom as long as we never forget that humanity is not the centerpiece of creation.

About the Authors:

Joe Strykowski is a marine naturalist and distinguished photo-journalist with more than 10 books and 500 articles which reflect his commitment to the ocean environment.

Dr. Rena Bonem is a professor of geology at Baylor University. For the last 20 years, her research has emphasized reef development in highly impacted environments.

Since 1975, they have worked in close association — developing and teaching coral reef ecology courses for educators worldwide.

Together they have explored and studied coral reefs all over the world gathering the material on which *Palaces Under the Sea* is based.